A Lawyer's Tale

A Lawyer's Tale

George Bridge

To order additional copies of this book, contact:
Xlibris Corporation
0-800-644-6988
www.xlibrispublishing.co.uk
Orders@xlibrispublishing.co.uk
301210

CONTENTS

A Child's War

CHAPTER ONE

Young Emily was well wrapped up in her warm woolly coat as she played in the sandpit with her brother Stephen. She was only just three years old and he was nearly two and looked very much like a little German boy in his shorts and leather braces. He was very playful and uncontrollable and suddenly he left his sister and ran over to an old man sitting on his own on a park bench nearby, and without any invitation he took the old man's walking stick off the back of the bench and began happily running around with it as though he had seized a trophy of great importance. The old man smiled when the pretty lady on the next bench apologised to him. She was clearly the boy's mother and probably Italian with those big brown eyes. Sometimes he wished he was younger.

"They are so full of energy at that age," he said to put her at her ease. "I feel quite jealous sometimes." They both laughed. He must have been about seventy years old and looked every inch the proud retired German businessman with his close-cropped grey hair and clipped moustache.

"Yes," replied Clara cheerfully in her impeccable German, "but they must learn to behave at some time—and perhaps that is such a pity because I just love them at this age!" She sighed and smiled at the old man who was clearly in sympathy with her and being very friendly. Since his retirement and the death of his wife he had enjoyed his daily walks in the park and always hoped for chance meetings with such charming people and it seemed strange to him that there was this new regime in the country to despise foreigners and he hoped it would pass. This lady was charming and clearly enjoyed her family life and bringing her children to the park and she too seemed to enjoy conversation with strangers, but then the Italians had always been sociable people and loved to talk.

Clara turned to Stephen and told him in her loving way that he should be a good boy and return the stick to the nice old man, which he did with a happy smile and then promptly ran back to his mother for a cuddle.

"Where are you from?" enquired the old man with a friendly smile, genuinely interested—as though he hadn't already guessed—and looking straight at Clara with his wizened old eyes peering at her from under his black Homburg hat. She was a very beautiful young woman with long dark brown hair and those big brown eyes which could only be Italian.

"I am from Italy—from Rome—but my husband is English from London" she explained. "He is an English teacher here".

"Does he speak German as well as you do then?"

"Oh yes", she smiled back at him. "We both learned a little before we came here and this is our third year here, so we are both improving all the time, and of course the children have no difficulties speaking German with their friends in the kindergarten all the time. David is only worried that their knowledge of English will suffer even though we do try to teach them English all the time. You see they don't speak any English with their friends, and we shall probably be returning to London soon." She didn't want to take the subject any further as she knew all about the threats of war looming.

"Yes, I suppose so if that is where he is from," he replied.

"He went to work in Rome first five years ago where we met, and after a year we married there and Emily was born soon after that." She explained, looking lovingly at her little girl still playing quietly by herself in the sand pit. She adored her children and was very happy to be out in the park with them.

"You must both be very good at languages then?" the old man was saying almost to himself but still smiling at Clara, and she began to wonder if he was flirting with her. Anyway she liked the attention, and he was being very polite letting her talk about herself which she also liked.

"My husband David was always good at languages, and went to France first when he left his job in England. He has always worked for the Berlitz School—perhaps you know it? The teachers only speak to the pupils in the language they are teaching, but of course they are also learning to speak the language of the country they are living in as well. He was in Lyons for three years and then he went on to Italy and we had a lovely time in Rome. I think we would still be there but his brother Edgar was working in the Berlitz School here and suggested that they swapped jobs. So Edgar went to Rome and here we are!" She smiled as though she had come to the end of the story.

"Well I hope you will be very happy here," smiled the old man and he began to rise on his stick to make his departure.

"Auf wiedersehn!" he said to Clara as he raised his hat and bowed slightly to her as he was taking his leave.

Clara put Stephen back into his pushchair and taking Emily by the hand she walked them back to their little flat where she knew her husband would soon be returning from his work and would want to find some tea waiting for him. As they walked along the pavement Clara did not take much notice of the other people in the street but she could not help noticing that every day there were more young men wearing those military brown uniforms. Some of them were shouting political slogans which she did not understand as they meant nothing to her. It was all just part of the atmosphere in the New Germany.

It was 1939 and the Nationalist movement was gathering in size and importance, and it was not even necessary to read the newspapers or listen to the wireless to be well aware of the brewing political storm which was gathering over Europe. The German army had already moved into some of its neighbouring countries and adjoining states, and there was a rumour that Hitler was about to announce the annexation of the whole of Austria to be part of Germany. The younger members of the German population were jubilant at the rapid growth in importance and size of their Fatherland, and they were quickly forming groups and units of the Hitler Youth Movement and proudly wearing the very distinctive brown uniform. They had numerous meetings in public places where the speeches became more aggressive and their nationalistic songs became more strident and offensive to other races and other nation states. They were in a high optimistic frame of mind and feeling very strong and aggressive.

David came home early from school that day as he did not have any late pupils and he enjoyed going straight home to see his children before they went to bed. They always spoke a mixture of German and English in the family which was very confusing, but David was very patient with the children as he knew that they would soon work it all out and then have the benefit of speaking two languages equally well.

He poured himself a lager beer as he spoke to Clara:-

"Things are getting serious," he said, and she just frowned and waited for him to go on. "There will be a war you know, and then we shall probably have to leave the country quite quickly".

"Is the nationalist movement so strong then?" she asked. They were speaking in English now and that was always a sign that David was trying to make a serious point. Otherwise they jumped from Italian to German as they were both so keen to improve their German.

"Yes, I am afraid so, liebling," he explained quietly, "they are even insisting on speaking strictly in "hoch Deutsche" in the school as though we were all part of their precious Fatherland!"

Clara heard him in silence as she never liked to believe the worst about anything and she was sure in her heart that all the troubles would just blow over and leave them alone to enjoy their family life in peace.

"Shall we go back to Italy if there is trouble?" she asked quite innocently. She did miss her family.

"Oh no my darling, I'm afraid that we won't be able to do that now!" David replied emphatically, "Didn't you know that your Mussolini has joined forces with Hitler? They have made a pact of some sort against the British, so it looks as though all British families will have to go home soon."

"Where will we live if we go to England?" asked Clara.

"We shall try to find a place near my sister Ruth in Tolworth," he replied without hesitation. "She has lived there for years now, so she is bound to have lots of friends who can help us."

Clara knew that when they moved to England it would be their last move as a family, but she enjoyed family life and adored her children, and so as long as they were together she did not really mind where that was to be.

The next day was just like any other and the children came bouncing into their bedroom at the crack of dawn to wake them up, and David was groaning as usual for them to leave him in peace until he gave up the fight. The children were excited that morning because there was a military band right outside their building, so David gave up the struggle and half-heartedly listened to the strains of the more and more familiar tunes of the marching anthems of the Nazi Youth Movement to which they were being subjected. He closed the windows with disgust and got dressed. He was in a bad mood already.

David read the news avidly every day, for although he was clearly in the wrong place at the wrong time with a war looming between his present country of residence and his home country, he was not quite sure where he wanted to go next. He had no home in England and he was virtually a nomad having been travelling abroad for over six years now. He had been very much in love with Clara when he first met her in Rome when she was a beautiful young woman, but after living with her for five years he was feeling differently, and he was angry inside himself with her flirtatious ways, and he was sure that when he was working at his school she was seeing other men when the children were in their kindergarten. He had no evidence of any of this, but he just had a very strong feeling that all was not well with his marriage.

David did not have many friends in Leipzig as he found that teaching was a very solitary occupation, and most of the English teachers were already leaving Germany to return home so he just continued in his work feeling more unhappy about the developing political situation. He knew that he would have to return with his family to England soon and he hoped that his sister Ruth there would look after them. If there was a war, then he would be called up and be separated from his family anyway, so he worked out that as soon as they left Leipzig they were probably finished as a family and he had better look after himself. It was just a matter of when that would be. He did not want to force a separation from his own children so when Clara asked him what they were going to do, he just continued giving her vague answers. He really didn't know, but he did worry about it because his colleagues at work were being asked to go home and it was just a matter of time before someone would ask him to move on and leave the country.

David was not a man of decision, and he actually did nothing at all and was still going every day to teach at his school when the announcement was made that England had declared war on Germany. The local police had been given a list of the names and addresses of English families living in Leipzig, and they called to find Clara at home with the children. They explained the situation to her in a very polite manner and said they would return the next day when they made it clear that they expected to find the man of the house at home.

David knew what was coming, so when Clara told him what had happened he stayed at home and opened the door to the three smartly dressed policemen who had been sent to see him.

"I believe that you are an English family living here. Is that correct?" asked the senior officer sternly in very formal German.

"Yes we are," replied David in a friendly and co-operative manner.

"Are you aware that your country has declared war on Germany?" went on the police officer.

"Yes I am," replied David in his best German "but what does that mean to us?"

"It means that you must leave Germany immediately, and you have been given twenty four hours to leave the country or you will all be arrested! Special trains have been arranged to take all foreigners to the Hook of Holland so please arrange to be at the railway station as soon as possible! You have until tomorrow night!"

The police officers did not wait for any reply but just clicked the heels of their shiny high boots and then disappeared down the stairs.

"Twenty four hours!" Clara went into a panic and burst into tears. The children were both crying in unison at seeing their mother so upset, and David tried to calm them all down.

"Now come on then," he said, "All we have to do is to sort out all we can carry and do as they say, then we shall all go down to the railway station!" He knew this was coming, and he was mentally prepared for the hurried departure.

The flat became a bustle of suitcases and packing and sorting out the few things they would be able to carry and the many things which would have to be left behind. Stephen was sitting on his beloved rocking horse and imploring that they should take it with them, but with no success. He also had to leave his teddy bear, but Emily was more lucky with her request to take some of her smaller dolls. Most of the books had to be left behind as were the lovely linens and kitchenware which they had collected over their travels. Clara suddenly became very realistic and made no objections, as she had also for a long time been made aware of their position in the community by many of the people she had spoken to in the street and in the shops, so she was in no way disillusioned or depressed by the final outcome of the inevitable situation. It was just that she had put the danger into the back of her mind as she was enjoying their family life and being with the children so much. The fact was simply that they were foreigners in a country at war and they were not wanted. Now she was only worried about her family and prayed that it would be held together, but she was having serious doubts as David was continually making comments about having to "go to war" and "join up" as soon as they arrived in England. Where were the family expected to go? How would she be able to look after the children? Everything seemed to hang on David's reliance upon his sister in Tolworth even though she had a family of her own. Was her house big enough to take them all? Clara had been brought up to put her faith in her husband so she trusted that David would look after everything.

Emily clutched her favourite doll tightly to her while her mother made sure that Stephen did not wander off and get lost in the crowd on the station. David was struggling with the luggage, and it was only with considerable difficulty that they all managed to board the crowded train taking them to the Hook of Holland. No one knew what they would find when they arrived at the seaport. The children played happily in the corridor of the train and soon became tired, so when they arrived at the Hook there was little chance of them running away and getting lost. They stayed close by their mother and hung onto her.

There were thousands of people rushing about trying to find out about the boats and how they should obtain tickets to board them. David told Clara very firmly that she should stay put with the children so that he could go and find out the position and then return to them when he had some tickets. The children were happy at first playing around the piles of suitcases which were on the station platform, but soon they became too tired even for this, and they just dropped down next to their mother and slept on the platform. Clara waited patiently.

David's brain was whirling. What should he do? Did he really want to go back to England and then be called up into the army? Did he want to keep his family together? Wasn't this the opportunity for him to start a new life somewhere else? He had done it three times in his life already, and there was nothing for him in England. He could always have another family.

There were many very helpful people at the Port Office, and David soon found that all the boats were going to England, so he believed that his fate had been established even though he may lose his family in the crowds. Clara would not know where to go to get a ticket, and even if she got to England she would not be able to find his family in Tolworth which she had never met or shown any interest in. So he took his boat ticket and went on his own to join the crowd of people who were waiting to be let on to the first boat. Clara would never find him in the crowd.

Clara waited for over two hours and then her Italian patience wore out.

"I am waiting for my husband to come back with the boat tickets for us all to go to England!" she explained to one of the many officials who had noticed her alone on the platform with her children and offered to help her.

"How long have you been waiting?" he asked, and when Clara told him, he took her and the children to the booking office and they were ushered straight to the front of the queue.

"This family has been waiting for over two hours for their father to be issued with their boarding tickets. Do you know what has happened to him?" he asked the clerk who was busily issuing the tickets and taking the names of all those who were given one. He told the official that he had indeed issued a ticket to David Richards, and where they should find him waiting for the boat and he promptly issued further tickets for the family. David was soon tracked down, when he immediately became flustered and made some excuse about finding room on the boat before returning to collect the family. Clara was furious, and suddenly understood the position she was in with her husband. At least she had her children with her and she was a survivor. David had already hinted that he would be leaving them to go to war, so she was mentally becoming adjusted to being alone with her family, and she would look after her children whatever happened.

CHAPTER TWO

The sky was grey and miserable that day in Tolworth, but it was Autumn and war had just broken out so no one was surprised at anything. All the family had arrived at last and were standing together in front of a typical English terraced house in a typical London suburb and the houses were all identical for as far as the eye could see. David knocked on his sister's front door which seemed to echo up the quiet street, and when Ruth opened it she was clearly delighted to see her brother standing there and she hugged him happily and made him welcome. Then she did the same to Clara and greeted her and the two children and ushered everyone into the small back parlour. It seemed as though the house was crowded with people, but they were all the family crammed into the parlour which was also the kitchen, and it was soon evident that no one ever used the front room unless it was a Christmas lunch or the vicar ever came for tea—which was always a family joke as they were all atheists. The vicar would never call and the front room would never be used.

Ruth had four children of her own ranging from four to ten years of age who soon pulled Emily and Stephen away from the grown-ups and into the back garden to play.

Tea was served on the parlour table with sandwiches placed on the clean table cloth and the discussion revolved around the journey home and the state of the war. It seemed that so far there had been no fighting or enemy action and it was all talk on the wireless, but Ruth's husband Albert was the first to be realistic and spoke out:-

"We shall all be called up into the army now," he said. "I suppose you know that Edgar came back from Rome last week and has already joined up? So I'll not waste any time and I'll go and join tomorrow."

They all nodded solemnly in agreement, and David turned to his brother-in-law to declare his support.

"I'm with you," he said. "Perhaps we should go together." They all nodded in agreement with the fact that it was inevitable that they should go.

It was soon arranged that the young children would all double up and share beds, and that a friend would be asked to put up Clara while things were being sorted out. David would sleep on the settee so as to be ready for an early departure in the morning with his brother-in-law.

There was a feeling of excitement and anticipation in the house that night as so many things were happening at once and everyone knew that the men were going off to the war in the morning. No one knew when they would come home again. The children were not at all aware of the seriousness of the situation, and they were enjoying playing games of tickling each other under the shared bedclothes. It was all a great game. They all slept well, and in the morning after a hurried breakfast David went round to see his wife at Ruth's friend's house. Secretly he was happy to be going to start a new life, but he did not want to give that impression, nor did Clara want to give away the fact that she knew very well that he was happy to be going and not having to be saddled with all the responsibilities of looking after his family. She was angry with him but would not let it show. She would be better off without him and soon be able to work something out. He would see how capable she was.

"Goodbye my dear," he said to her by the front door. "I must go now but I shall let you know as soon as we are told where we are going and when. Look after the children won't you?" and he was gone with a quick peck on the cheek.

A few days went by before Clara appeared at Ruth's front door to ask for her children. Her sister-in-law was clearly embarrassed about something, and Clara guessed that she had had a long talk with her brother before he had left to go and sign on with the army, and she probably knew that things were not going too well with their marriage, but was too tactful to interfere. She was a good and kind mother and knew that little Emily and her brother Stephen would have to go with their mother.

Clara had not wasted any time during those few days while she had been staying up the road, and she had been making enquiries and discovered that she could move into an empty house nearby which she had agreed to take over as a tenant. David had not re-appeared or contacted her so she had taken advice and gone straight to the local Authority to seek financial assistance. It was all very distasteful, but ever since the episode on the dockside in Holland she had lost all faith in her husband and had come to the conclusion that she was fighting alone for her welfare and that of her two small children. She would show everyone that she could manage on her own. She was nearly twenty four now.

Emily and Stephen enjoyed playing in the road outside their new red-brick house as there were many half built houses in their street and plenty of lovely new bricks to stack together. The builders had simply left everything to go to war and there were piles of bricks and building materials all over the place. Life was tough for Clara, but she was beginning to enjoy the challenge of finding her way in strange waters and she soon succeeded in claiming money from the Local Authority to keep her two children. Her English was good enough to converse with anybody, and she had the added advantages of being an attractive woman and also having the Italian characteristic of not being afraid to talk to anyone and everyone. On reflection she enjoyed the thought that these were both qualities which her husband did not possess as he tended to be shy and typically uncommunicative. He would see that she could survive without him. It was just that Stephen was a bit of a handful and she was always trying to find someone to take care of him while she was job-hunting or shopping with Emily who was much easier to control.

The weeks and months went by and Clara moved from one job to another and continued to collect her assistance from the Local Authority, but it was all a bit much for her with two children. Air raids were now being made over London which was very frightening and her life was very difficult, so when she heard about the evacuation plan to take young children out of London, she applied for Stephen to be included. Then she would only have one child to look after which would not be such a handful. She loved Stephen and promised him and herself that she would go and see him regularly wherever he was, but at least he would be properly looked after out of danger and she could get on with her life and hope to earn a better living with more time to spare.

Stephen was four years old and could not understand why he was with all those crowds of children on a platform at a big London railway station being put on a train going to somewhere in Devon. He was wearing a luggage label on his coat with the address of his destination written on it, and he was carrying a gas mask over his shoulder. Clara cried as she waved him goodbye and she promised that she would visit him when she could. She loved him like a mother and he would have to understand. Everyone was crying and kissing. Stephen suddenly realised that his mother was sending him away on his own and he began to cry because he didn't understand why. Someone was given the task of putting him off at the correct station where he was met and taken with a few other young boys in a smart family car to the house where they would be staying.

The house on the edge of the quiet Devonshire village was a huge manor house which was owned by a senior diplomat who was helping the war effort abroad somewhere, but he had agreed with many others to join the government's new scheme to keep his house open and arranged for the staff to stay on for the benefit of a number of young children to be evacuated there so that they could be moved out of London and away from the danger of bombing raids. Stephen found himself with six other young boys, all of about the same age who became like a new family under the supervision of a firm but kindly woman who they all called "Tiger". She was nothing like her nick name and adored the boys, but she ruled the house with a rod of iron, and the boys soon learned about the importance of discipline in the most kindly of ways. They loved it there and soon got into the routine.

There was a convent school nearby, and Tiger drove them there every day where they learned to read and to write and do many other useful things. Stephen enjoyed everything new and especially making baskets out of coloured raffia which they were given to do. One of the nuns was quite a good teacher, but she was known to be a bad disciplinarian, and the children soon became aware of this and took advantage of her by playing childish jokes on her without fear of any punishment or reprimand. This soon came to the notice of the Superior Sister who told off the whole class and told them to behave.

"If I see any of you children leaving the room during Sister Jane's class I shall make the culprit stay on after lessons!" she told them very severely.

It was a basket-making day in the class, and there was a lot of moving about to fetch and carry pieces of raffia and Stephen was trying to push past Sister Jane's chair when he said quite innocently, "Will you excuse me please Sister?" Without any hesitation she replied "Well of course Stephen, but don't be too long dear," when he realised to his horror that he had been misunderstood and that she had thought that he wanted to go to the toilet, so now he had to go there even though he did not need to, as he was far too shy to explain the mistake in front of everyone.

As soon as he went out of the door he saw the Superior Sister in the corridor just waiting to see if anyone would come out as part of a joke on the poor teacher.

"Now Stephen," she said kindly, "What did I tell you?"

Stephen looked glum, and just felt that it was all too difficult and complicated to explain his error and that he had not meant to come out at all, and that he had certainly not intended to play any jokes on the nun whom he really liked. So he said nothing and was told that he would have to be punished and stay on after the class was over. The Superior Sister could not have been kinder when taking him for the extra lesson and Stephen warmed to her immediately. In fact he enjoyed the episode of being taken notice of to such an extent that he asked for more special lessons to improve his writing skills which the Superior Sister was pleased to give him and give him a head start on other children of his age. She had felt his eager response to her teaching and found a willing pupil who very quickly improved his reading and writing skills, as he asked again and again for her special attention and extra time which she was pleased to give to such an enthusiastic young boy. He would get on and she would see that he went on to a good preparatory school when he left them.

Back in London, Clara had left the house in Tolworth where she had always felt uncomfortable since David had left her and his sister had shunned her completely. She received occasional letters from David who was with the army in Egypt now, but these were really meant for Emily because he was missing his children. Clara had decided to take the advice of a friend soon after the bombing raid started and she moved to Shrewsbury in the midlands where he had a friend who needed someone to look after an empty shop which had a flat above it. Clara was to look after the premises and live there rent free. She was going to enjoy being out of London and away from her husband's family which had let her down so badly and had not done anything to help her. She had been brought up in a country where the family was paramount, and members of a family always helped each other out, no matter who was arguing with whom. She was sad to find that this was not the case in England.

Clara realised that her move would mean that the children should go to a boarding preparatory school nearer to her, so that she could go and see them when she was not busy and they would come to her for all their school holidays. She wrote about this to David who was happy to oblige, so long as he did not have to do anything or to pay any bills. He had been given a commission in the Intelligence Corps because of his knowledge of languages and the army would look after his children's education bills. He just continued writing his letters every week to his children and supposed that they would remember him when the war was over and the time came for him to go back home. In the meanwhile he was having a good life in the Headquarters of his Army unit interviewing prisoners with his knowledge of German and Italian. He was with the Eighth Army and there was a good spirit among his colleagues in the officers' mess in Cairo.

Back at home Clara had found a good preparatory school in a village in Shropshire not too far away from Shrewsbury, so the children would be able to come home to her at weekends. She collected young Stephen from the lovely house in Devon and when he had made all his sad farewells from his friends and the staff there, they made their way back to London where they collected Emily and then went on to Shropshire and the new preparatory school. Stephen was hoping that he would at last be able to have some time to play with his sister as he had missed her, but this was not to be, as the boys and girls were separated into different parts of the school, and they may as well have been at different schools.

Stephen hated the place immediately, as no one was nice to him like Tiger had been in Devon. There were no treats like the cakes the cook used to give him when he asked nicely. All the young pupils were just ordered around and no one seemed to care about him at all, so he was very sad and miserable. After a few days he met his sister in the playground, and she was also very unhappy about the place as it was the first time she had been away, and they both cried together. Suddenly Stephen remembered that Mummy had said that if they were not happy they did not need to stay at the school, so he put his arm around his elder sister and said that they should leave the place at once.

They agreed to meet at the gate after school and without a word to anyone, they made their way in the dark down the road. Neither of them would have done it alone, but together they were fine and all they had to do was to find a telephone to speak to Mummy. Stephen had no idea how to use a telephone so he was very impressed and proud of his sister when she got into the telephone box by the roadside and spoke to the operator who put her through to Mummy who was fortunately at home. She asked where they were and then told them just to wait there for her. It seemed to be a very short time before she suddenly arrived with a friend in a motor car and took them home to Shrewsbury.

It was not long before Clara had found another prep school in the area for the children in the town of Oswestry, and although they were immediately separated as before, they quickly made friends and settled into their new life in different parts of the school.

The headmistress was one of those kindly middle-aged ladies who knew exactly how to treat young children and to make them obey her without any fuss or rancour.

"Please read out of this book for me Stephen," she said pointing to a page and thrusting the book into Stephen's hand. He did so without any trouble or hesitation and the teacher realised that he was well ahead of his years and would do well at the school with his work. He was sent off to join a small dormitory and was soon exchanging stories with his new schoolmates.

"You were born *where?*" asked one rude little boy incredulously. "Germany! Are you a *spy?*" and Stephen was mortified, but the name stuck, and he was bullied slightly by the slur. He held up well though, and fitted in with the other boys although he became a bit of a rebel in trying to prove himself and was often punished one way or another. All of the teachers were young ladies, and one of them often gave Stephen a beating when he was naughty. That was Miss Morrison. She was very pleasant to the children and Stephen especially liked her geography classes where he learned about other countries, and all about where the war was being fought and where his father was. When Miss Morrison punished him it would be just before bedtime when she would take him to her room and tell Stephen to take down his pyjama trousers. Then she would smack his bare bottom with a ruler two or three times. It never really hurt much, and she always stroked his bottom afterwards to be sure she hadn't done him any harm. Stephen liked that but he was too young to feel any embarrassment.

Then one day the headmistress sent for Stephen.

"Your father is here to see you!" she said, and there was this tall bald man in uniform who looked just like the photos which he had of him, but he couldn't really remember him, as he hadn't seen him for four years which was more than half his lifetime. It was therefore with mixed feelings that he greeted his father, and David tried hard to get closer to his young son by producing a present he had brought for him all the way from Egypt. He held out a long leather camel whip and gave it to his young son who was thrilled to receive such a present. The headmistress smiled and said that she would find a suitable place to hang it on a wall until Stephen left the school when he would take it with him.

David stayed to have tea with the headmistress and then took Stephen for a short walk in the town. This was another new experience for young Stephen who was not normally ever allowed out of the school grounds. He felt very strange being with his father, who was a complete stranger to him but he tried to understand that this was the man who wrote to him every week from wherever he was with the army. It was all very strange to the young boy who was anxious to get back to play with his friends.

David was enjoying his first leave home and as soon as he had returned his son to the school, he went back to the railway station to go and see his wife in Shrewsbury. He knew this would be difficult, but he hoped that time had healed their differences when they parted. He had also been doing much thinking about their relationship, and decided that he was not ready to just throw away his marriage. He would try again, even though he was unhappy about having to travel so far to see his sister's family in Tolworth and then to have to make his way up to the Midlands to see his wife and children. He would therefore try to persuade his wife to return to London and to keep the family reasonably close together. His motives were entirely selfish because Clara had made a nice little home in Shrewsbury and had a good job as a French teacher at a local boys' school.

The children stayed on at their prep school and both did well and enjoyed it there. At half term all the pupils went home to their parents for a long weekend and Emily and Stephen loved going home to Shrewsbury. It was therefore quite a shock to Stephen when one half term his mother asked him to stay at school and she would only have Emily at home. What did she think Stephen would feel like? He had done nothing wrong, so he was mortified and never forgot it. He cried himself to sleep in the empty dormitory and became much closer to the headmistress who understood exactly how he must have felt and therefore invited him to join her in her private part of the school house. Stephen was asked to read passages from good English literature to her father who was permanently in bed, so again his education was to benefit by some trick of fate.

Stephen was an adventurous lad and was always looking for something new. He often misunderstood things as he did not have the benefit of parents to teach him the basic facts of ordinary life, and on one occasion he was trying to understand what made electric lights work. He had been told many times not to go near any electric points especially with wet hands, so his curiosity was aroused even more, as he could not understand the mystery. Suddenly there he was standing up in the bath drying himself after having a hot bath in the small bathroom, when he noticed that there was an electric socket in the wall right in front of him and well within reach. What would happen if he put his wet fingers into it? He had been told that electricity was dangerous, but he did not know why, so he tried it. The electric shock he received threw him out of the bath onto the floor, and the mistress who should have stayed with him ran back into the bathroom and gave him a good scolding. The young lad should have been killed, but somehow no damage was done except for the extreme shock from which he soon recovered.

Soon after that experience, news came over the wireless that the Italians had surrendered, and the school mistresses could be heard running about the place shouting with glee to each other. "Now only the Germans to beat!" they were screaming.

"Will your mother want to go home now?" Miss Morrison asked Stephen jovially, when Stephen realised that he had not even thought of that possibility, so he could not reply to her. "Don't worry," she went on "She wouldn't want to leave a lovely boy like you!" but it made him think that there was a possibility that he may be left alone one day.

They were soon on holiday again in the Shrewsbury flat, which the children liked mainly because of the empty shop downstairs where they could play with the many clothes which had been left there, and they could dress up and play childrens' games to their hearts' content and not bother their mother upstairs. She was happy in the flat which had two bedrooms and had a good view into the picturesque town looking one way out of the window, and to the bridge over the river Severn looking the other way. Clara could speak to anyone in the street from the window and she used this method to speak to anyone who rang the front doorbell. Shrewsbury was a friendly town and she was soon on speaking terms with many of the neighbours who soon knew all about her. It was a good friendly atmosphere.

Donald was one of her many admirers and he would just ring the bell when he was on leave and passing by. He was in the merchant navy and Stephen loved to see him in his sailor's hat and bell-bottomed trousers. He always played with the children and brought them sweets and small presents. Clara thought he was like a breath of fresh air around the place. Stephen adored him and that made her happy too.

"Mummy I want to be a sailor!" he declared one day when he was nine years old, and Clara knew that Donald had made a good impression on him. She knew nothing about Donald though, and for all she knew he could be married to some lucky lady in Portsmouth! The war was like that. She never took anyone really seriously and never allowed any man to stay with her in the flat when her children were at home.

The children were at home when the Germans surrendered and the town went mad on that spring day in 1945. There were noisy celebrations and fireworks, and the singing of happy crowds could be heard everywhere late into the night. Clara didn't mind staying in to look after the children, but she kept the windows open so that she could join in by shouting down to the happy people in the street below. No one cared that she was Italian and that her country had been on the other side. She was British now, and she was enjoying it. She had made so many friends there and Italy was just a fond memory.

Another era was coming to an end and both Stephen and his sister had passed entrance exams to go to good secondary schools also in the Midlands. David had done his homework and found that there were many schools to choose from now that his children had both passed their entrance exams, and now that the army was paying the necessary fees he could send them to good boarding schools within a reasonable financial limit. Emily would therefore go to a friendly looking place near Droitwich and her brother would go to a good Grammar School in Worcester. So once again they would be close to each other but probably never see each other except on holidays.

David found himself in Berlin at the end of the war so he decided to stay on there and transfer to the Control Commission of Germany. It was an easy transition for him as the job he would do would be virtually the same he had been doing all through the war—interrogating German prisoners, but instead of finding out about Nazi troop movements he would be asking them about Russian espionage. The cold war had begun and his life would continue undisturbed, and he could look after his children from a distance and see them when he liked. This would not be too often because he now had a German girl friend and it suited him down to the ground that one of the rules of his position was that he was not allowed to marry a local citizen. Fraternisation they called it, so he just let Lisa move in and be his housekeeper.

The end of the war had been a cruel business because so many people had suffered and been killed that the victors wanted to take their revenge, and the decision to let the Russian troops take Berlin was a cruel one. That was one of the decisions made between the Allied commanders and political leaders at the Yalta Conference after the war on the basis that Russia had lost many more men in battle defending their country than any of the other combatants. They would therefore be allowed to take their revenge on the civilian population of Berlin.

They completely destroyed whatever was left of the city, and the young women were made to feel the pain and suffering. Lisa was no exception, and she felt lucky to have survived at all. She had lived for over two years under the rubble of her old family home in the centre of Berlin which had been destroyed by the bombs. During that period she had stolen and begged for food for herself and her mother and daughter who were living together with her in the rubble in those disgusting conditions without water or toilet facilities. It was a complete struggle for survival which they always thought they would lose especially in the bitterly cold winter months. Somehow they survived, and it was no secret that Lisa and many of the attractive young

German women would sell their bodies to the marauding Russian soldiers at any opportunity in exchange for food or clothing. Her daughter was too young to understand what was happening, and her mother was too old to be of interest to the young soldiers. When it was all over and the city was divided up into the four sectors she was so pleased to have been found by David that she would do anything for him. She never again spoke of those horrendous months because somehow she felt that it was her own country which had precipitated the world into that Second World War when they should have learned from the lessons of the First.

CHAPTER THREE

David's interest in his children in England was a very distant one and he began to appreciate that the little young Italian wife he had married in Rome had grown up and was well able to fend for herself and look after the children. He had to pay bills from time to time, but with the government support he was receiving, this was no great hardship and he was able to run his own second life in Berlin at a very acceptable standard. There were many privileges granted to members of the forces there, and to the government agencies like his own, and he felt like being in a colony in the middle of a wilderness. They had their own currency and their own NAAFI shops and could buy many items of food which had not been available to the local residents since the last years of the war. Cigarettes and coffee were at a premium as were other luxuries and therefore transactions were frequently made to exchange any old family heirlooms and treasures which could be found, for the necessities of life. The occupying forces were taking their revenge.

Back in England Clara had taken David's advice and moved to London where she had been offered a flat in one of those long streets of terraced houses in the residential suburb of Finsbury Park. She found she could fit in anywhere and everybody loved her. She knew nothing of David's new life, and still thought after their short time together in Shrewsbury when he came over for his short leave, that they would get back together again when he left the army. So she stayed in the new lodgings for over two years waiting for him to come back, with the children coming to stay with her for their school holidays. Eventually David wrote to her and told her the truth and she hated him for it, but ever since she had been in England she had always felt that their marriage was over. Anyway she had made her own way without him, and somehow that had given her a strength which she may not otherwise have had.

Clara was a very positive minded person, and when she got over her anger she made a point of meeting new people who would give her ideas for a better future, and as an attractive young Italian woman she was never short of admirers. So she moved from place to place, and every time the children went home for a school holiday they seemed to be going to a different address. It was fun for them and of course they never missed what they had never had—a real home or a real family life.

Emily was very happy with her new school and soon made friends there and she enjoyed the atmosphere generated by a bunch of adolescent girls who were far removed from their homes and from any of the bad influences of living in a big city. They worked a little and played a little and generally had a good time in a way which was considered to be the best grounding for young ladies who would either marry shortly, or perhaps go into one of the more genteel occupations in society. Very few of them passed any exams.

Stephen was quickly thrown into the rough and tumble of a boys' boarding school life. He was just eleven years old and went into the boarding House of his new school with a few other new boys who were immediately surrounded by the ruling older boys of the House.

"Can you box?" he was asked by an older boy who was trying to find competitors in every weight for the House competition. Sport was clearly paramount to their existence, and Stephen was anxious to participate in anything new. He didn't know what he was good at, so he decided to sign up for everything—even boxing, where he would learn the hard way what it meant to fight his own corner. It was all fun, even if it was sometimes painful.

The Boarding House stood on the ground of an old Convent which was apparently there before the Reformation in the sixteenth century. There was an old tunnel from the boarding house to the city cathedral which had long since been filled in, and the new boys were always treated to the doubtful story of the nun who had been trapped in the tunnel and died there, and how her ghost appeared on the night of every full moon. Many new boys suffered from nightmares and sleepless nights before they became accustomed to their new home and passed on the stories to other new boys.

The principle extra-curricular activities were sports orientated, so even though the school appointed a master for each sport, the Housemasters were unrelenting in spurring on their own House teams for each and every sport. So while one evening one of the House masters would be there coaching the House rugby team, the following evening the same master would be showing a group of youngsters how to pull their weight on a tug-of-war rope. The boarding House prided itself in turning out well-mannered boys with all the necessary social attributes, so Sunday evenings were devoted to holding mock debates in the dining room where every boy learned the art of public speaking. Another evening was devoted to ballroom dancing, and even masters who were notoriously always bachelors, showed the young boys in the gym how to do the intricate steps of the quickstep or the tango to the music of Victor Sylvester being played on a wind-up gramophone sitting incongruously on a sports bench. The boys would not have their chance to practise these steps with a girl until they were in the sixth form, but it was all good training and few of them forgot the steps they had learned by the book. Stephen loved it all and used to practise his dance steps whenever he found himself alone in the common room of the boarding house and the right music was blaring out of the old radio stuck in a corner.

Every day as soon as school was over all the boarders went straight back to the boarding house, and if there was no game to be played, they immediately changed into running togs and go for a training run up the canal bank, extending the distance of their run every day. There was no supervision for this, but every boy knew that he was expected to do his best to keep in top form of fitness for whatever sport he participated in. The end result was shown by the many trophies which were won by the boarding House. They always seemed to be better than the day boys because of their ruthless training and enthusiasm. There was another very subtle inducement, and that was the board of honours which every boy wanted his name to be inscribed on. This was a board which was produced every year and hung in the dining hall with the names of all the boys in the House of that year on it showing their sporting achievements. These boards were the talking point of many meals, and every boy wanted to earn some letters to be put by his name before he left the school.

There were many pranks played by the boys and some of them got into more trouble than others and found themselves standing outside a prefect's study after prep waiting to be beaten with a slipper by one of the prefects for some misdemeanour. Stories of many previous House prefects had become legends with their power of the slipper. The prefects ran the discipline of the House and it seemed to work very well. The Housemasters kept their eye on what was going on but never interfered. The boys all knew their place and how to behave, this created a strong bond of camaraderie as each boy tried to get on and improve his position in one sport or another. There was very rarely any bullying—or if there was, it was quickly and effectively stamped out, and Stephen was fortunate in being at a school where there was absolutely no drug-taking or homosexual activity. Some of the older boys took up smoking and went to cafes in the town to do so, but they were careful never to be seen smoking on the school premises as this was an expulsion offence.

Stephen fitted in very well with the other boys and tried all the sports he could, but there did seem to be something missing in his background which no one could put their finger on and which probably led to his often unruly behaviour. He was beaten for these incidents like everyone else, but there was more to it as he went through a long period of wetting his bed during the night which no one could understand. Everyone was very sympathetic and left him in peace to wash his own sheets every time it happened, but the fact remained that he was probably emotionally disturbed, and no action was taken by anyone to attempt to cure the problem. After a year or two the problem just went away but no one had dealt with it or its causes. Stephen was very much alone in his private life as however much his mother loved him she was always away somewhere and however much she wrote to her little boy, she could never give him the love and affection he badly needed. She had her own problems and was doing well to survive at all moving from place to place and from job to job. There was nothing secure about her life, but wherever she was she tried to maintain contact with her children and wrote to them every week. She worried so much about Stephen that she began to send him her food ration card, so that once a week he could at least go out and buy the cream buns which he could just afford to buy out of his small pocket money. Clara always found a way of getting the little food she needed to live on.

Stephen was very happy at school and soon fitted in with all the sports and other activities. Also he found that he was always in the top strata of his class, and he knew that he would probably pass his exams when the time came. He was also included in most of the extra-curricular activities even though he was not particularly strong or well built. He was just enthusiastic and a good team boy.

The main problem for Stephen was in the holidays, because he was no longer his mother's little boy, and although she looked after him, she virtually ignored him and did not know how to talk to him when he was with her in all those different bed-sitting rooms for those school holidays. Then Clara began to go back to Italy to see her family in Rome and when she did this she arranged with David in advance that he would have to pay for the children to go and stay at some holiday home or hostel while she was away. Some were very good and provided good facilities for the children to play in large gardens, but they were never like a home—which neither Emily nor Stephen had ever known anyway. None of the family ever cared for them or even wrote to them, although every once in a while dear old Uncle Edgar appeared out of nowhere to take them out. Stephen relished those visits especially, probably because Uncle Edgar never forgot to slip a half crown piece into his little hand when they parted.

The Boy Scout movement came to Stephen's rescue as an extra-curricular activity when a group of Sea Scouts in Worcester of all places (being so far from the sea) invited members of the boarding House to join them at weekends and to take part in their adventures on the River Severn which ran through the city. Stephen went for it enthusiastically as he went for everything else, and it was not long before they introduced him to another branch of Sea Scouts near his mother's latest bed-sitting room in London for him to have something to do in the holidays also. From then on his spare time on holidays was completely taken up with their activities, and Stephen was then always going off to take some test of seamanship or Boy Scout activity, and he was ultimately awarded a King's Scout certificate by the Chief Scout in the grounds of Windsor Castle over a very special weekend. This was a great achievement but no one came from his family to support him or to congratulate him, but he did not expect this as they never came to see anything he did.

Back at school, when the time came, Stephen was made a House prefect and was given certain privileges such as being allowed out of the school grounds for one evening every week to go to the cinema. This was a momentous starting point in his life as he had never before experienced such freedom—even for a few hours. The school rules had been relaxed recently to allow prefects to own their own bicycles, but Stephen did not have any money to buy one, and his father was giving him less and less now, so he told his mother how he felt left out. Clara was also not in the habit of giving her children presents as quite simply she had never had the money to do so, but she was never lacking in initiative, and she saw that there were advertisements in the newspapers by people selling such things second hand very cheaply, and replied to one for a bicycle being sold in Dorking for thirty shillings, so Stephen set off with his sister by train one weekend to collect it. That bicycle remained his pride and joy for the remainder of his school days and made a fundamental difference to his social life from then on.

Stephen was growing up quickly, but his determination to be a sailor had not left him, so he asked his housemaster whether he could take the entrance examination to Dartmouth Royal Naval College. The housemaster was very willing to help a boy who knew what he wanted to do even if that meant helping him with ancillary subjects—such as in Stephen's case where he would be examined on a fixed syllabus of English literature which went beyond his school curriculum where he was specialising in science subjects. Stephen reported to his housemaster's study every evening after his prep time, and was put through his paces on the set works by Milton and Shakespeare, so when the exams came in he passed them all with flying colours and was sent for an interview at the Royal Naval College. He only had to stop once on the way for a quick medical examination in London, but he did not worry about that as he knew he was very fit with all the sports he had been playing at school.

He took the underground to a part of London on the East India Dock Road which was totally unknown to him, and which was taken up mainly with dark and dingy warehouses and massive cranes along the parts of the River Thames Embankment which were still being used as commercial London Docks.

"Just look at the small spot of light you can see in the mirror in front of you," said the kindly doctor who was examining his eyesight.

They were in a darkened room, and Stephen could clearly see the spot of light in the mirror, but he was baffled by its colour so he guessed:-

"Green—I think," he answered. There was an ominous silence.

"Try again," said the doctor quietly. "And take your time"

Stephen knew then that he was wrong and panicked. "White?" he tried.

"I shall leave you for a few minutes for your eyes to become accustomed to the dark," and the doctor left the room. It was eerie. Stephen had never been questioned over his ability to recognise colours before, so it was all a bit of a shock for him.

The doctor returned after what seemed an eternity, and he started to flick different coloured lights onto the mirror, asking Stephen each time to give the colour. He only used three colours: red, green and white, and still Stephen was getting them all wrong. He tried with larger and smaller spots, but it was no use. Seeing those lights in total isolation, Stephen could not tell which colour they were, and yet in normal life he experienced no difficulty in perceiving colours, and he actually enjoyed painting in his art classes and playing with coloured flags with the Sea Scouts.

"I am afraid that you have a problem with your colour vision, and I cannot pass you to go on to Dartmouth for your interview!" he said very definitely.

Stephen was shattered. He was already thinking of himself as a budding Captain Horatio Hornblower R.N. and going home to his mother proudly with gold bands on the sleeves of a smart naval uniform!

"What shall I do now then?" he asked the doctor lamely.

"Oh go into something else! You won't have any problems at your age," the doctor replied nonchalantly, "but I have to send you back to your school now."

Something else! Stephen thought about this and realised that he had never considered any other career as he had not visualised that anything would stop him going to sea and becoming a naval officer. He cried on the train and felt that his life was shattered. Why hadn't anyone taken enough interest in him and in his health to the extent of even testing his eyesight? So he returned to school and informed his housemaster of the problem when he was greeted by a similar response, but with a little more sympathy.

"Now you can go on to take your A levels and think about going on to university if you want," he said, and Stephen sloped off to his study feeling very dejected. He was beginning to become very fond of chemistry as a subject, but he did not see where this was going to lead him. He was also well aware of the fact that the reason he really like chemistry was because the chemistry master had put such faith in him when everybody else had treated him like a rebel. This faith led to Stephen working very hard to prove himself which he did very well and in turn this resulted in him being elevated to be a senior school prefect. He could even be School Captain the following year. The only fly in the ointment was the arrival of a new headmaster who tried to make immediate changes to some of the very old traditions of the school. This was anathema to Stephen who regarded the old traditions as sacrilege and he was not tactful enough to by-pass the new head's proposals without causing him offence, and soon he had made a real enemy.

Some of the new headmaster's ideas were quite practical, as for example his idea to let the boarders learn something about gardening on a Sunday afternoon when they really had nothing to do except go for a walk. Those walks had however been the only opportunity for the boys to stray outside the confines of the school other than for their sports activities which were strictly controlled, and for the senior boys they were the only real opportunity for them to meet any young school girls who may also be taking their walk up the river bank or elsewhere. It was easy for the prefects to present the new idea to the younger boys as one which was not approved of, and none of the younger boys would dream of doing anything which the prefects did not recommend. The headmaster was not a stupid man, and soon realised that his ideas were being torpedoed by the older boys, so the sooner he could get rid of them the better it would be for his absolute control of the boarding house.

Stephen was now sixteen years of age and Emily nearly eighteen, so their father David thought that it was about time that he invited them to come over to Berlin for a summer holiday. He had to introduce them to his new partner Lisa sooner or later, so this would be as good a time as any, and he thought they were about the right age to understand that as enough years had passed since his divorce from their mother, he was moving on to another life with another woman. The Control Commission paid the fare for the children, but he would have to arrange for the accommodation. Emily could squeeze into their flat and he arranged for Stephen to have the use of a spare room of a neighbour upstairs in the same block of flats. Both Emily and Stephen were very excited about the trip and took the boat train to Calais and then a special train from there to Bad Oynhausen in Germany. They had to wait there for a special train to take them through the Russian "corridor" of Eastern Germany as Berlin was still behind the "iron curtain". This was very exciting for all the children because there was very much a "cloak and dagger" atmosphere between the East and the West, and even though the train was a special one for school children visiting their parents in Berlin, they were locked in their compartments and an armed Russian guard patrolled up and down the corridor of the train.

Stephen and the others in the compartment loved all this, and they immediately pulled back the curtains of the compartment to look out of the window at the black darkness of Eastern Germany and shone their torches into the nothingness, flashing morse code signals at absolutely no one. This was adventure! Then when they were escorted in groups into the buffet car that they found that they could buy tins of Benson and Hedges cigarettes very cheaply which they had heard they would be able to exchange with Germans in Berlin for amazing things like cameras and other valuable items. Stephen bought a few tins just in case this was true.

David enjoyed having his children with him in Berlin and he wondered why he had not done so before. They enjoyed everything he did for them in their different ways and he even taught Stephen how to drive by letting him drive his own Volkswagen motor car in the quiet streets of the Grunewald district of Berlin where he had his flat. In a way he was too liberal with his children, because it was not long before Stephen with his adventurous spirit had found his way to the Kurfurstendam, the main street of the city, and was allowing himself to be picked up by the ladies of the night who were quick to seize upon the fact that he had some cigarettes in his pocket. He was learning fast, and more than anything else he enjoyed to see the young beautiful German girls wearing their sexy clothes in the street and relished the way they came up to him and spoke to him in English even if it was only to find a way to separate him from some of those lovely cigarettes.

Neither David nor Clara had taken it upon themselves to explain to either of their children any of the "facts of life" as they both assumed that this would be taken care of by one of the many boarding schools their children had attended, and to a large extent this was true, as both Stephen and Emily soon found that wherever they went, their peers were only too anxious to share with them their thoughts and experiences connected with the opposite sex, but this method of learning was always rather crude and explicit—especially in Stephen's case where he found himself being secretly shown with lots of giggles the most explicit sexual photographs and lude nudes by his chums who were not averse to sharing their bouts of masturbation with their friends, but this never extended any further and Stephen was never subjected to any homosexual behaviour. He was introduced to this in a roundabout way by noticing boys at other schools behaving in a strangely intimate manner towards each other when he visited those other schools to play rugby or cricket. It was all just a joke to him and his friends, none of whom ever showed any interest in sexual deviations.

In Berlin David took the children on a yacht on the lovely Wansee lake in the middle of the city, and Stephen enjoyed showing off his sailing skills to the family which he had learned from the Sea Scouts at home. Emily and Stephen often crept across the road to peer through the fence of the Spandau prison camp where Albert Speer the last of the Nazi war criminals was being kept imprisoned for the rest of his life but even though they never actually saw him it made a good story to tell their friends at school. It was all an exciting experience for the growing children, but soon they had to return to England and go back to school to their schools to finish their studies.

As a prefect of the boarding house, Stephen enjoyed the privilege of being allowed out of school for one evening every week and as none of the boys had any family anywhere near the school, it was assumed by the masters that all the prefects did with this privilege was to go to one of the cinemas in the town. The prefect would then write the name of the cinema and the film on an "exeat" slip which was left with the housemaster each time. Stephen had to find out from another prefect every week about which films were showing as he did not go to the cinema at all. He needed an alibi as had met a lovely girl from the town at one of the sixth form dances and she was inviting him to visit her at her home in the town every Friday evening.

Janet was a lovely black haired girl who was just nineteen years old, but she was already working full time at the city's main telephone exchange, so it was easy for Stephen to telephone her at any time during the day. She was happy to have Stephen as her boy friend, and she asked her parents to go out to the cinema every Friday while she entertained him at her home, and there she taught him everything about the pleasures and art of making love. They didn't do much else. She was a lovely sexy girl and relaxed with him, so their love-making got better and better. They were both sensual creatures and enjoyed giving pleasure to the other. Janet as the older and more worldly-wise one, was also quite sensible about what they were doing and ensured that Stephen always used a contraceptive and then took it away with him at the end of the evening when they knew her parents would return, always at about the same time. Stephen then happily cycled back to school throwing the used contraceptive into the river as he crossed the bridge. The routine worked like clockwork and Stephen was becoming very fond of Janet and thought he would go on seeing her after he left school.

He never knew what affect he had on Janet, but their relationship was very beautiful and mutual as she had great respect for Stephen. She knew that he would go on to achieve many things and she was very proud and fond of him. She hoped that when he left school they would find a way to stay together as he was just the kind of boy she would really like to marry. In the meanwhile she enjoyed his sensual kisses which always made her go weak at the knees and made her feel very sexy. She felt his immediate responses to her and the first time they had kissed she had felt his hard maleness pressing into her and she had wanted him and made all the necessary arrangements to keep her parents out of the way so that she could invite Stephen into her home and do everything with him as she had always dreamed. She decided to take him over and keep him as a special boyfriend and enjoy the relationship which she wanted to go on and on. For Janet this was a very special and serious affair as she thought that Stephen was out of her social league, so she did not invite him to her home when her parents were there. It was too early for them to talk about living together, but she knew that it would happen one day if their relationship progressed as well as it was doing. She loved him and always looked forward to his telephone calls which she knew he could only make from a telephone box in the High Street, as there was no telephone in his school boarding house.

The school organised many trips abroad for the boys which were well organised and filled in some of the holiday gaps for Stephen when he had nowhere to go, and so he was invited together with his studymate Hassan to join such a party which was going to Dublin. When they arrived there, they were allowed to wander about the lovely city and soon they met a friendly group from a girls' school in Manchester. Stephen and Hassan made friends with two of the girls who showed that they were interested in them and in their boarding school life and asked them all about their strangely cosseted life. They were shocked to hear how they had to stay confined in the boarding house for their half term holidays as both their parents were abroad and they had nowhere to go.

"You should come and stay with us for your half term!" declared Yvonne.

"My mum wouldn't mind and we have plenty of room in our house, and Pam is just round the corner—aren't you darling?" she directed to her friend who was sitting close to the Iranian boy and who nodded enthusiastically.

"Just tell us when you want to come up," she aimed at Stephen, obviously being very sincere about her invitation.

"Thank you," replied Stephen and smiled politely. "If you really mean it, I don't think we are doing anything for next half term in November. But you must ask your mother first, and then write a formal invitation to us. In fact I think it may be better if you wrote your letter as though we were going to stay at a hotel, or our headmaster may object as he doesn't know who you are," he said, and Yvonne agreed to comply with his request.

It was all a perfectly innocent invitation and no "hanky panky" was likely in the circumstances, or even intended, although Stephen and his study mate did like the girls. Stephen was very pleased when the letter of invitation arrived and he told the headmaster that he and Hassan would be going to Manchester for the half term weekend to stay in a hotel there. The headmaster believed none of it because he had intercepted the mail sent to the two boys and knew about the plan, but he said nothing and let them go. He then immediately informed the police that the two boys were under his care and that they should be apprehended and brought back to the school.

The parents of the girls were dumbfounded when they opened the door of their house to find a police officer standing there, but they believed that they should stay out of it and leave the boys to explain the mistake to the headmaster, and so the boys were escorted back to the school. There the headmaster told Hassan to go to his study and he turned to Stephen and immediately accused him of being deceitful.

"You lied to me when you said that you were going to stay in a hotel weren't you? You were going to stay with some girls!"

"It isn't like that!" protested Stephen. "We were invited by the parents to stay at their house, but we thought it would look better to you if we said we were going to a hotel rather than a private house."

"You admit it then—that you tried to deceive me. I am legally responsible for you while both your parents are abroad and you should have told me everything."

Stephen was boiling inside because he knew that the headmaster would never have given him permission to go and stay with complete strangers, but he was perplexed as to why, if he took the matter so seriously, he had not telephoned his father in Germany who would certainly not have objected to Stephen accepting such an invitation. He was clearly prejudiced against Stephen and had made up his mind that it was all a wicked plot to deceive him.

"And I know that you have been seeing someone regularly!" he exploded, "Is it the same girl—eh? I have seen you using the telephone in the High Street!"

So that was it! There was no telephone in the boarding house, so any telephone calls had to be made from a telephone box in the High Street which meant walking past the headmaster's house and being seen by him, and he had the kind of mind that guessed that as Stephen had no family in the area, he must be telephoning a girl friend and in his mind that was a terrible sin.

He told Stephen that he was being expelled immediately and that he had to leave the school the next day before the other boys came back from their half term holiday and he was to go and stay with his Uncle Edgar in London who had already been informed. Stephen heard later that Hassan was not blamed at all but was given six strokes of the cane for being led astray.

Stephen was shattered and upset at this catastrophic change in his life and the next day he meekly boarded the train from Worcester to London for the last time. The noisy old steam train didn't feel the same as it had always been with his chums going home for holidays, so he sat there in the compartment and cried quietly until a young lady sharing the compartment (who turned out to be a nurse going home for a break) spoke to him and engaged him in conversation for the rest of the journey. He felt a lot better then, but the fact remained that his school days were over. He had never known any other life having been sent from one school to another since he was four so the world suddenly seemed to be a very big and strange place that he knew nothing about. He was a truly lost soul.

Uncle Edgar now lived in a flat in central London with his new wife Alice. He had kept up with Stephen and Emily by visiting them from time to time in different parts of the country over the years while his brother was unable to do so, and somehow Stephen always felt close to him because he was such a kind man and always brought him little presents which meant so much to him as it was more than his parents did! He had recently married Alice who was lovely and everyone loved her and Stephen was now going to live with them both in their flat.

This was the first time that Stephen had ever lived with a couple, and he was old enough to feel very guilty about being thrust upon them in this way as though he was a criminal, and he felt another guilt that he was interloping upon a lovely new and happy relationship. They welcomed him with open arms and couldn't have been nicer though, so he said nothing about moving on and out of their way. He wondered what they thought about the incident at his school, as it seemed strange that they never raised the subject except to insist that Stephen should speak to his father on the telephone about it on the very first day. That was a terrible conversation as Stephen did not know what to say to his father who did not seem to want to support him at all and implied that Stephen should apologise to him for the fuss and bother. Stephen never forgave him for that lack of support, and the little self-confidence which he had built up slowly at school with the help of his chemistry master and a few others was now totally shattered.

Uncle Edgar was starting a travel business, and as he and Alice were looking after Stephen like a son, they took him with them wherever they went and Stephen just did what he was told to do in the office happily sorting out replies to newspaper advertisements and stuffing brochures into envelopes and addressing these to go out to potential clients. They all knew that he was waiting for his call-up papers to go into the army as was every boy of his age, and as Stephen was always feeling guilty about overstaying his welcome in their household he expedited his call-up by making a telephone call to the appropriate department of the War Office.

Clara was still in Rome with her relatives, as she was so often in those days and sister Emily had moved into a flat with friends in another part of London. Stephen was looking forward to Christmas that year when his father would come over from Berlin for the first time with Lisa and they would all be together in Uncle Edgar's flat. In the meanwhile Stephen was enjoying a new kind of real family life which was added to by the kind attention he received from Alice's family who were all perfectly normal and had a great sense of humour. They were fun and Stephen enjoyed their company and even went to stay with them when Edgar went away on business and thought that it would be more correct for his wife not to be alone with Stephen in the flat.

Alice prepared for a big Christmas party that year, and all the cousins came—even Edgar's mother who was over ninety years old and her own mother who was a bit younger. There was only one spare bedroom so David would have that with his German partner Lisa who Stephen had met on the one holiday he had spent visiting his father in Berlin. As soon as he arrived at the flat with Lisa, David noticed the close family bond which had built up between his brother and his son Stephen, and he was very jealous of this because he had never been able to get that close to Stephen, as a result of living abroad for so long. This made him angry and so he confronted Stephen late one evening, when Stephen had been having an amusing conversation with his uncle, by asking him rather aggressively :_

"Don't you know who I am?" Stephen was nonplussed by the outburst and replied:—"Of course you are my father", whereupon David replied "Then why don't you treat me with some respect!" as though he had been hurt.

Stephen thought for a moment and replied almost to himself, "I don't think I was ever taught how to speak to a father."

David turned and sullenly went to bed and never raised the subject again.

An Army Story

CHAPTER ONE

King's Cross Station was alive with hundreds of potential passengers hurrying to find their trains. Many of them were anxious looking young men looking for their train to Catterick Camp in Yorkshire where they had been ordered to report for the beginning of their two years compulsory National Service in the army. Barry found a seat in one of the third class compartments and soon realised that most of his travelling companions were other young men who had also been called up. The engine was belching out great clouds of steam and sounding an occasional whistle as though to hurry all the passengers along to find their seats and settle down for the journey. The compartments were rapidly filling up with lots of young men who were all following orders contained in similar letters to the one Barry had received from the War Office telling him precisely where to report and when. The letter had also enclosed a postal order for one day's pay in advance and the travel warrant to pay for the journey. He had never been paid anything in his life before, except for the weekly pocket money he received at school, so he was really thrilled by that and promised himself to keep the postal order and frame it one day.

Most of the passengers on the crowded train were about eighteen years of age and seemed to come from all walks of life. The two years of National Service they were going to begin had been a part of every young man's life since the Second World War, and most of them had different views about it. Most fathers were happy to see their sons go out into the world and be taught some real discipline by someone else, and at the same time be shown other parts of the world at the tax-payers' expense, while most mothers were sad to see their sons being taken away from them—except for those who were tired of trying to control a badly behaved son, in which case she was happy to see the State taking a hand in developing the boy's character without making any impositions on her. As far as the boys themselves were concerned, most of them just took it in their stride as part of the adventure of growing up, but some who were dedicated to starting an early career elsewhere were annoyed at what they considered to be a waste of time. Some of them had managed to have their two years removal from their studies postponed until the end of their university course or even to avoid doing their National Service at all. Many would live to regret that, as they were missing an opportunity of an adventurous new life being offered to them on a plate free of charge.

Barry was one of those who was very keen to start his National Service, but he also felt the need to leave his uncle and aunt for whom he thought he had been a burden as he hated the feeling that he may be a nuisance to anyone even if they had not said anything to imply that he was, so he was happy to be going away and to be starting his own real life. His uncle had been very good to him and showed more interest in him than his own father, and he thought of his last words to him as he left him on the station:-

"Don't forget my boy, that you have had the benefit of a much better education than most of the chaps you will meet, but many of them will be just as intelligent as you, if not more so, so have respect for everyone you meet."

His life had needed a kick start, because no one had been interested in what he was going to do. Both his father and mother were far too busy with their own lives to be bothered with him, and presumed that his school would sort something out for him to go on to, but in fact his school had no system for helping boys with their careers and presumed that it was the parents who would guide their sons along a chosen pathway. So no one cared, and Barry had just drifted on with his education without any idea of where he was heading. He would probably have gone on to some secondary university if his headmaster had not taken a hand and told him in no uncertain terms that he should leave school. Barry didn't like him at all but he had that power and his father did not care enough to intervene, so perhaps it was a blessing in disguise.

The guard blew his whistle and the train was on its way slowly chuffing out of the station and into the grimy northern suburbs of London. Barry felt relieved that a new life was beginning and looking out of the window he noticed the rows of blackened houses so close to the railway line and the rather sad number of washing lines which must have been gathering all the soot and black dust belching from all the passing trains. The atmosphere in the packed compartment was quiet and sombre as most of the young men lit up their cigarettes and puffed away in silence. They all looked new to the experience of going away alone, and none of them knew what to expect at the other end of the train journey. They needn't have worried, as the army had been making arrangements for the handling of new recruits since time immemorial, and their induction procedures were practised with a fine art and catered for no nonsense from any of the new lads who may have thought that he could have ideas of his own. They would soon learn that any ideas they may have had should have been left at home or wherever they came from.

At last, after several boring hours of rushing through the English countryside, the train pulled into the small railway station for Catterick Camp in the depths of Yorkshire and disgorged its passengers of hundreds of bemused young men. Suddenly they were being shouted at by several sergeants and corporals immaculately dressed in their army uniforms who were in charge of the reception arrangements and who had been waiting for the train on the station platform. They knew the drill and were not going to leave any doubt in the minds of the new intake of conscripts as to who would be in charge of their movements from the minute they arrived.

"All new recruits make your way into the transport lorries outside the station!" they all shouted, as they guided the helpless looking young men who were wandering up the platform wondering where to go. The three-ton lorries were soon full up and making their way out of the station car park and along the narrow roads to Catterick Camp and to "7 T.R." which was the famous basic training regiment for all new recruits being enlisted into the Royal Corps of Signals.

Barry found that he was enjoying the experience of a new and exciting adventure as he had been rather unceremoniously pushed out of his boarding school and sent to live with his uncle and aunt, who were very kind to him, but he thought it was rather unfair being forced upon them as a newly married couple simply because his parents were too busy doing their own thing. It had always been like that. His father had taken a job in Berlin after the war in the Control Commission as he really had nothing to come home to. He had divorced Barry's mother several years ago and now had his new German girl friend who looked after him very well. Barry's mother spent most of her time shuttling between her work looking after her business of keeping two bed-sitting room houses in the Bayswater area of London, and travelling to see her Italian family in Rome. As a result of this neither of Barry's parents had ever thought seriously about buying a family home for their children who were therefore thrown from pillar to post in their school holidays. They knew no other way of life and fortunately both of them had enjoyed their school days and made their friends there. Every one of their school holidays had been a separate adventure and sometimes they saw their mother and sometimes they didn't. They just got used to it and sometimes the arrangement worked out well and they found themselves in very good caring company, and sometimes they felt that they were totally abandoned. It was just the luck of the draw and without them realising it, a very good character building exercise—even if a little lacking in warmth and affection which both parents seemed to think was just a natural phenomenon—although both of them did think that they were entitled to undying love from their children . . . but that is another story.

Here was a sudden change in Barry's life and he realised that for the first time he was on his own in the world, and this was no holiday. He could see from the expressions on the faces of all the other recruits who were reporting with him that most of them felt more lost and abandoned than he did, so he took every opportunity to make some kind of a joke with anyone who was near him. Twenty of them were now standing in a group in the chilly doorway of the sparse Nissen hut waiting to be allocated one of the meagre small iron beds around the walls of the narrow tin hut. He soon fitted in with most of the other young men as he had been accustomed to do over the years in his boarding school, and he immediately made friends with many of his colleagues sharing the hut, many of whom were sadly missing their home lives where they had been spoiled by their mothers.

Alistair was given the bed next to him on which he unceremoniously dumped the blankets, linen, army clothes and other articles which he had just collected from the stores and looked at Barry in bewilderment.

"Och a wee!" he exclaimed with disgust. "They think of everything d'ya noo?" giving away his obvious Scottish background.

"Yes I guess they have quite a workable system by now!" agreed Barry with a smile, and they both began to sort out their many items of clothing on their respective beds while the hut gradually filled up with other recruits doing the same thing. Suddenly there was a huge shout from the doorway:-

"Stand by your beds!" and one of the corporals who had heralded them from the station was standing there looking daggers at anyone who was still moving.

"You must be the scruffiest lot of idle individuals I have ever had the misfortune to set my eyes on!" he screeched at them.

"Somehow me and my colleagues have got to turn you shower of crap into a unit of soldiers within four weeks—and I must say that I have never had a more unlikely task put my way! Stand still when I am talking to you!" he shouted at one poor individual who had moved slightly from one foot to another. The corporal walked over to the poor lad who was obviously feeling very uncomfortable at having been picked out for no good reason, and he put his face only about two inches away from the new recruit's nose. Then he turned and screamed at all of them:-

"While you are here you will do as I say, and follow my orders or you will be wishing that you had never been born! Do you understand?—I said do you understand?"

There was a quiet reply from them all of "Yes corporal" until the corporal repeated for a third time "Do you understand? I didn't hear you!"

"YES CORPORAL!" they all shouted back in unison. They were getting the idea.

"That's better!" the corporal replied. "Now then," he went on, "You all have your own lockers next to your beds for the kit which you have just been issued with, and I want you to put it all away and make up your beds, but before you do, watch me carefully and I shall show you how it is to be arranged on your beds every morning for inspection by the duty sergeant. Gather around! Come on, come on!"

The young men all crowded around the chosen bed-space and watched the corporal with amazement as he rapidly but carefully folded all the blankets and sheets into a stack at the head of the bed so they looked like a large block of mixed ice-cream. Each item had been folded to have exactly the same width. Then he worked his way down the bed putting every item of the issued clothing in a particular space, finishing at the bottom of the bed with three pairs of grey woollen socks which were each folded into immaculate blocks which he made look so easy to do. Then he left them to practise what he had just done and left them with the command to be sure to do the same with each of their bed spaces the next morning.

Alistair made some joke about the whole thing, but was soon practising making up his blankets so that he would be able to do it more quickly the next morning. Barry thought that to be a good idea and soon they were improving upon each other's attempts and laughing at their progress. Some of the others didn't think it so amusing as they had made up their minds that they didn't want to be there at all. They were going to rebel about everything, and Barry felt for them, because he could see that there was little point in bucking the system and probably getting hurt in the process.

Later into the night Barry could hear some of them crying in those small iron beds. Then the next day the sullen and resentful ones were soon getting into trouble not only with the corporal who had been put in charge of their hut, but also the other non-commissioned officers who were now totally in charge of their lives. It did not pay to cross them and risk the penalty of some obscure extra duty—like scrubbing out a toilet with a toothbrush or whitewashing a pile of coal. Anything was possible in the minds of those malicious young corporals who were really enjoying their almost infinite power which they had been given to discipline the new recruits. At least once every day they would be sure to pick out someone who had not polished the brass fittings on his belt sufficiently, or another who had answered him back when he had given some obscure order, and then a punishment would be given to the unfortunate culprit to show all the others that it was not worth rebelling against their authority, and so discipline was strictly maintained.

There were rumours spreading about really bad corporals in other huts who abused their powers and used physical violence against some of the recruits, but Barry never saw anything so untoward or any actual illegal or bullying behaviour. As far as he could see all the punishments which were given were well deserved. He kept himself out of trouble so as to avoid the punishments—even though he was occasionally picked out for potato peeling duties or other unsavoury activities which had to be shared between them all. The corporals and sergeants in charge of the new recruits seemed to have been hand-picked for the job, as they seemed to relish in giving obscure punishments to ridicule the culprits, but it was all part of the regime of bringing some of those unfortunate recruits down to size and make them understand their true position, which was equal with all the others.

There was a rumour in the camp that the tea they were given (which was plentiful from the canteen) was dosed with bromide to reduce the normal sexual stimulus in young men and prevent any misbehaviour of that kind, but Barry saw no evidence to support this except that it did seem curious that there was no attempt to break out of camp to find dates with the opposite sex or any homosexual conduct in the huts. If it existed it would have been all too evident in those close quarters.

The elements of basic training were taken very seriously in the unit, and most of their methods had been cleverly worked out to bring out the best in young men over the shortest period of time. The instructing corporals and sergeants clearly set out to break their spirits and then to build up a proud loyalty and allegiance of the new recruits to their unit, and the entire army which was second to none and based entirely on strict military discipline.

One clever manoeuvre was to issue each of the men with a new battle dress with a smart white insignia of the Royal Corps of Signals on each shoulder, but this could not be worn until the passing out parade in four weeks time. It was therefore hung on a coat-hanger above the bed and kept well pressed by its owner without ever being worn, and the white letters were carefully whitened again and again in readiness for the big day when the immaculate uniform would be worn with pride for that parade they had all been drilled for day after day for a month, after which all the men would be allowed out of the barracks for the first time for their first home leave.

In the meanwhile the men spent all their days in their working dungarees and being ordered about from one training lecture to another. At least twice a day there was a tough and exacting drilling exercise on the parade ground. The training was strict and ruthless and any slackers were quickly ordered off to the Guard room to repent and think about mending his ways. Every half hour or so during training exercises there was a break which was clearly designated for smoking which was almost compulsory as there were no other forms of relaxation available, and they could not stray far away in the short time available.

"Left! Right! Left! Right! Move to the right in threes, right TURN!" screamed the drill sergeant, and so it went on with different variations in the drill, and the men were becoming smarter and more and more disciplined without them even realising it. Staff-sergeant Crabtree was a legend and infamous in the regiment for his strict discipline and control of the new recruits. He knew what he was doing after so many years practise, and after a week or two under his command on the parade ground the men were taking it in turns to give the orders. It all worked impeccably, and the different platoons were soon vying to be the best for the passing out parade. This was their only goal and it was working every time. A pride was built up in those men which was second to none and they were soon arguing in good spirits between themselves as to which of the platoons was the best one.

Eventually it was Barry's turn to be interviewed by one of the administration corporals whose job it was to determine where all those men should be sent to after their basic training had been completed.

"Now then," he said looking at the papers in front of him, "You are Barry Edwards, aren't you, and you appear to have three "A" levels on your School Certificate. Do you realise that qualifies you to apply for a commission—would you like to be an officer?"

Barry hadn't given it a thought, with all the rigours of the training and fierce discipline, and suddenly he realised that he was being given a choice to go up in the world. This was new territory and he liked it.

"If you want, you will be sent to another regiment when you return from your home leave for eight weeks pre-OCTU training. They will then decide whether you should be sent to an Officer Cadet's Training Unit at Mons or Eaton Hall providing you are selected by WOSB—which is the War Office Selection Board. So you can see that there will be a lot of extra training and work involved and of course there is no guarantee that you will pass or even be selected. Do you want to give it a try?"

One thing Barry had been taught at his boarding school was to face up to challenges, and this was a new one, so he knew what he had to do. After all, he thought, what was the point of being in the army for two years if he didn't try to meet the challenges which were thrown at him? He had nothing to lose and he had already noticed the miserable attitudes which were being adopted by some of his mates who were showing resentment to being called up at all for what they considered to be a waste of two years. This only made them unhappy and complain all the time, and that was not Barry's style. He would do his best, and if he didn't make it—well at least he would have tried. So he put his name down for the pre-OCTU training and knew where he would be going when he returned from his first home leave. That was a good feeling.

The day for the passing our parade approached all too slowly as every evening all the recruits continued with the same boring routine of sitting on their beds cleaning their best boots with spit and polish as they had been taught to do by their corporal and other old hands in true army fashion. It was the only way to make rough leather shine like glass and the lads even competed with each other to produce the best results. When eventually the big day arrived they had all made their plans to go home after the parade, and Barry couldn't wait to go back to his uncle and aunt for the weekend and show off his smart new uniform and shiny boots and tell them all about his new life. He had forgotten that his uncle had fought in the second world war himself and had been discharged with a serious wound many years before. He never mentioned it.

The parade went as smoothly as clockwork with every man putting his best effort into the drill movements in front of their Commanding Officer whom they had hardly seen during all their time at the unit, and who now congratulated them on passing out of their basic training and dismissed them, wishing them well wherever they were going to be posted to. He would have another intake to take care of on the following day. The parade was followed by a rush to the lorries for the railway station and Barry felt as good as the rest of them all dressed up in their new smart uniforms to go out into the world as smart new young soldiers. He smiled to himself as he thought of how cleverly the army disciplinary system was and how it had been built up over so many years. He thought of how in times of war the success or failure of it could mean the difference between life and death if a soldier hesitated on the battle field to obey an order, and the army was not going to change its ways now. Who knew what actions there were just over the horizon? What Barry liked was the visual affect of this philosophy. Every man had pressed his new battle dress uniform perfectly so that the creases in the trousers were straight and sharp, and their polished best boots glistened like glass. The khaki web belt around his waist was blancoed to perfection and the brass fittings on it shined like new. Every man was proud of his turnout and at every opportunity he would automatically give one or other of the brass fittings on his uniform an extra little rub.

CHAPTER TWO

Barry felt as though he had been away from civilian life for a year and not for only one month as so much had happened to him in that time. His uncle and aunt were very happy to see his enthusiasm when they welcomed him back home, and they could see that he was enjoying his new life and felt sure that he would get on well. There was a strength and determination there which was difficult to analyse, but it was almost as though for some reason he had to win some private battles for himself all the time. He often referred to his old school days and explained to them how it had been instilled into all the boarders at his school that they were expected by their chums to succeed in as many sports activities as they could. In the army he was finding that it was the same thing really, and the recruits in their training were always being challenged to compete with each other to do better than them, and to achieve that little bit more every time. It seemed to work and bring out the best in all of them—except for some of the worst misfits, who would usually be the same poor one or two individuals who just didn't fit into anything. Barry was fine and was always there with the leaders of the pack and would have done even better if he had been bigger built, but he had quite a small body frame and used this to his advantage over difficult obstacles on the assault courses. He was looking forward to returning to the camp and to his further training at the pre-OCTU regiment where he knew that again he would be competing against his new chums in a friendly spirit to aspire to being selected for a commission.

This time when the recruits arrived at the railway station they were taken to one side to be transported to "4 T.R." which was the pre-OCTU camp, and this time they were in their smart uniforms and looking much better than on their previous arrival. There was also a huge difference in their reception because this time they were all volunteers for the next stage of their gruelling training, and any slip-ups would be rewarded by them simply being returned to their unit, and this threat was always to be hung over them during their training.

At the new camp they were immediately allocated to their billets, which were a slightly higher standard than they had got used to in their basic training, and within minutes of their arrival they were being ordered around by very officious young corporals and sergeants who were over-aggressive and seemed to be deriving some pleasure out of their excessive reception activities. This went on for less than an hour when suddenly they all started laughing as they were informed that they were actually imposters, and that there was a tradition in 4T.R. for the latest outgoing recruits to make a scam (which was called "the Grip") for the new recruits, by borrowing uniforms from some willing genuine officers and non-commissioned officers who were well aware of the tradition, and pretend to be the reception staff for the new training unit. It only lasted a short time, but it always worked, because they knew that the new recruits would do anything to impress the new staff—even if they were imposters. They would do anything for fear of being sent back. The Grip was easy fun for those taking part.

"Stand by your beds!" was the command, and every man stood rigidly to attention while private Jones pretended to inspect his bedspace and the kit which had been meticulously laid out on the bed. Then he had to suppress a smile while he criticised the poor lad's kit or his turn-out. They were soon found out and became friends when the truth was revealed and the new routine was explained to the new lads who soon realised that in eight weeks time they would be doing the same thing to other new recruits, and that was something for them to look forward to.

They were soon introduced to the real corporals and sergeants who would be in charge of their training, and this time they also met the officers in charge and were told about the different regime and higher standard of training which they must pass to be recommended to go to WOSB and then on to Mons or Eaton Hall if they were selected.

Barry enjoyed the training and particularly the emphasis placed upon initiative and planning. He took his turn in giving impromptu lectures on subjects which were just picked out of the sky to see how the recruits would perform.

"Your turn Richards!" was the order from the sergeant in charge. "Speak for ten minutes on sponge puddings!" and Barry just had to think of something to say which was plausible and relevant. The sense of it all gradually began to take shape when related to men in action who needed to be kept informed about all kinds of subjects which may be strange to them wherever they were and the officers in charge must be able to explain things to them quickly and concisely to ensure that there was never any loss of morale. The British Army did not want to have officers who could not automatically take command in any situation and make decisions which his men would follow without question. It was all good character-building stuff.

Then on another occasion they were all asked to prepare a full one hour lecture on any subject which was of particular interest to them, and it was amazing how diverse the subjects were and how knowledgeable most of those young men were on their favourite subject. Barry chose photography as his subject, and explained in full detail how the size or aperture of the lens of a camera affected the depth of focus on the subject of any photograph. He made it all very interesting and illustrated his subject by taking photos of his colleagues which he then had processed and copied to give them all souvenirs later on.

Drill on the parade ground was still part of the training, but now the standard was raised by introducing elaborate drill movements in both quick time and slow time, and by making the recruits take over much more often, so that they became used to giving the correct orders in the correct way. Thus they were being prepared for their new role if and when they became officers and would be giving such orders on a regular basis.

The gruelling route marches got longer and longer, and soon they were doing twenty miles or more with full gear and more weights added to their back-packs. Then there were the assault courses which Barry thought must have been designed by a group of sadists as many of the obstacles were very cruel in their difficulty and were too much for many men who were often ordered to tackle almost impossible walls and scramble through dirty tunnels. The men were trained to be absolutely fit and then taught to recognise ways and means of achieving results in tackling difficult obstacles which only a few weeks ago they would have considered to be physically impossible.

Even though the training was much harder than the basic training had been, the men were made to feel that there was a definite pattern and objective this time, as there was no need to break any man's spirit or attempt to enforce his loyalty or enthusiasm because all of that already existed and could be taken for granted. Now the goal was much higher as these men were all aiming to be selected by WOSB and to go on to become officers in the best army in the world. They all knew that, and were often reminded that the pass rate by WOSB was less than fifty per cent and that was why the Royal Corps of Signals gave this pre-OCTU training as they wanted all their applicants to be within that top fifty per cent bracket.

There was a high standard in most of the sports activities too, as the men were so fit, but Barry was perplexed to see how his unit always seemed to come out on top of nearly all their rugby matches against other teams from all over the country, and in other sports too. He soon discovered that the officers on the permanent staff of the unit were not backward in coming forward, and that they made a practise of sending out "scouts" to find the best players in the good sporting schools in the land and to tip them the wink that when they were called up for their National Service, they should ask to be posted to the Royal Corps of Signals! The War Office were always happy to oblige, and did not realise that they were thereby giving one regiment in the army a distinct advantage when it came to sports activities—which was not something which exercised the top minds in Whitehall!

Discipline was maintained at a very high standard in the unit by both the officers and NCOs (non-commissioned officers), but this was exercised in a sensible way by them as they knew that they were dealing with future officers who could even be their superiors one day, and they also kept strict discipline for only the hours on duty, so there was plenty of room for recreation which was encouraged. Not only were there many opportunities for sporting activities but the men were permitted when off duty to go out to the village nearby or into Richmond and Darlington to explore the social possibilities there. Many of them soon found girl friends in the local dance halls and elsewhere, who knew from the white tab on their shoulders that they were training to be officers. That made them more eligible.

Barry was soon enlisted into the 4T.R. rugby team and enjoyed many good games against other regiments in the Corps without travelling far, as there were many playing fields in the camp, but he never aspired to play for the Corps top team as they were so heavily endowed with the international players who sometimes spent their entire National Service just playing rugby until they were free again to return to their rugby clubs in the country after their National Service had come to an end. Nevertheless Barry enjoyed the sporting activities and soon met a number of kindred spirits who became good friends, and often met them to go out on the town at weekends and enjoy their leisure time.

Sam was another aspiring cadet and he had a similar background to Barry and they often chatted together as they had been given the joint responsibility of being placed in charge of the armoury. This meant that between lectures and drill sessions they shared the responsibility of either one or both of them spending their time in the armoury to guard the rifles and other arms which were kept there for the entire regiment. Every time recruits needed their rifles they would draw them out for the drill parade or whatever, and then return them again after they were no longer needed. No rifles were kept in the sleeping quarters or other parts of the unit, but it all seemed to be a fuss about nothing, because there was no ammunition stored there anyway.

There were long spells in the camp when there was no activity, and so Barry and Sam would enjoy playing cards or other games in the armoury. To while away the time they had invented a new way of making toast which was to heat an electric iron and then spit on a slice of bread before holding it firmly against the iron for a matter of seconds. This produced a good quality of toast much to the amusement and enjoyment of all their visitors, as toast was one of those items of food which never seemed to be on the menu in the canteen.

The weeks dragged on towards the date of the appointments which had been made for each of the recruits to attend WOSB for their all-important application for selection to go on to Officer Cadet School. They were all well briefed by their friendly commanding officer with regard to the procedures which would be adopted in the selection process, and he told them that they should take an interest in current affairs as they would be subjected to several interviews for them to show their mental aptitude and suitability to be commissioned, and this would certainly include their knowledge of world affairs and world-wide politics. He took a pride in the high percentage of successes he had attained in the number of his cadets who passed the WOSB test and he was always trying to get them all through if he could.

The pre-OCTU training came to an end with a passing out parade, and although they were then all given a short leave, most of them stayed on for a few days and decided when they would take their leave as this could be at any time before they had to report to WOSB. So that was why there were many of them available to prepare the "grip" for the next intake of enthusiastic new aspiring cadets. Barry borrowed his uniform from one of the subalterns in the unit, and his colleagues had no difficulty in doing likewise from sergeants and corporals in the regiment who enjoyed watching the whole thing from a distance. They had taught the boys well and would enjoy seeing the results.

The new recruits lined up by their beds with the phoney corporal swearing at them at the top of his voice before he informed them that the duty officer was a real tyrant and scared them half to death! In due course he brought them all to attention and Barry swaggered into the hut trying to keep the smile off his face remembering how he had felt in the same position only eight weeks before. He made a pretentious speech to the new intake and then asked the "sergeant" to take them outside for a drill parade so that he could see how well disciplined they were or whether they should be sent back to 7T.R. This petrified the lot of them who were determined not to be shown up, so they each determined to put on a good show. They were formed up outside the hut on the road which stretched for miles into the Yorkshire Moors, and their "sergeant" gave the order.

"Quick march!" he shouted and followed up with an occasional admonishment to one or other of the new recruits to smarten himself up, before he just let them go on, and on, and on—until eventually the poor lads realised that they were on their own and the victims of a wicked prank and slunk back from the depths of the Moors to their barracks. When they returned angrily and feeling rather foolish to the camp, they met the architects of the prank, and soon calmed down when the grip had been explained to them, and they were appeased by the thought that they would be doing the same thing to other new recruits in eight weeks time.

The time came when each of them made their way to the WOSB unit in Surrey where they reported in and found themselves grouped together with the other applicants who came from military regiments from all over the country. They were each immediately given blank overalls to wear for their short visit, without any insignia to show which regiment they had come from, to prevent any bias or prejudice in favour of any particular regiment or against any others. The whole process would take three days, when they would be told whether or not they were being recommended to go on to Officer Cadet School.

Barry enjoyed the whole procedure immensely because every test was a challenge, and he intended to show his ability to face these with the colleagues around him. They were not in competition as there was no reason why all of them in his group should not be recommended. It was simply a matter of every candidate impressing the adjudicating officer that he was officer material. They took it in turns to make speeches and to give short lectures on some easy subject or another, but the greatest tests were the practical ones out in the field, when the whole group of five or six applicants were told to accomplish some physical challenge like crossing a stream with a barrel (or some awkward object) with the assistance of only two poles and a plank, or some other task, when they took it in turns to be the leader of the group. They were all fun and Barry enjoyed re-living his sea-scout days and he took a pride in helping whoever was the leader to find a way to complete his particular task.

On the third day of the tests, all the recruits had a last chat with one of the senior officers running the selection board, when several questions were asked about general knowledge and background, and then came the waiting for the decision to be made by those officers as to which of the recruits were suitable to be trained as officers for the British Army. When the time came for the announcement to be made they all stood in line to receive the verdict, when they were each handed a slip of paper which simply told them whether or not they had been recommended. They could keep the result secret if they wanted to, but none of those in Barry's group did—even though two of the five had not been recommended. It was all too emotional after all the training they had been through, so when Barry saw that he had been recommended he could not help jumping up and down with joy and relief. He was going on to Eaton Hall to train to be an officer.

Barry would have liked to go to Mons to train as in officer in one of the infantry regiments, but his medical test had shown that he was slightly colour blind, so that meant that he could only be commissioned into one of the supporting Corps and if he wanted to join an infantry regiment he would have to apply to be seconded to one of his choice in due course. All cadets training to be officers in one of the many supporting Corps in the army were sent to Eaton Hall, and that had many advantages as it was the old home of the Duke of Westminster in the County of Cheshire. It was reputed to be a lovely place within easy reach of Chester for evenings off duty.

It would be a few weeks before the next intake was sent to Eaton Hall, so Barry returned to his unit at Catterick Camp which had become his second home, and filled in his time by going on a typing course which he thought should be useful to him one day. He also read a lot of classical literature which he had never had time to read before, and he enjoyed going out in the evenings to say goodbye to the many friends he had made in the area which had changed his life so much over the past year. Now that he was definitely going ahead onwards and upwards, he was given a stripe on his arm to make him a lance corporal and he found that he was treated with a new respect, as some of the permanent NCOs were already calling him "sir"! He would get used to that, and from their viewpoint, they knew that there was a possibility that he could be posted back to them as an officer. He was not alone as Sam and others who had passed WOSB were also waiting to go on to Eaton Hall, and so they were all given various responsible jobs in the meanwhile like helping with the new recruits who arrived at 4 T.R. for their pre-OCTU training.

One day Barry was helping with a new batch of aspiring cadets who had just arrived, when he recognised one of them in the group who had been a school prefect at his school and had then gone on to university before doing his national service. So here he was, older than Barry but a year after him in starting his national service, so finding himself subject to Barry's superior rank. It was tempting for Barry to get his own back for the several injustices he could remember having received at the hand of this individual, but he thought it wiser just to let him know where he stood and not to take advantage of his position. It was satisfying just to feel that the tables had turned in his favour.

Eventually the big day arrived for the new cadets to report to their Officers' Training Unit and Barry took the same train as Sam to Chester to go on to Eaton Hall. When they arrived at Chester station he was interested to note the very different approach adopted by the NCOs waiting there to meet him from those who had met his train when he arrived at Catterick camp a year before. First of all it was a Sergeant-Major rather than a corporal, and the group of quite smart new cadets were being greeted far more cordially.

"This way please gentlemen!" was the command, and Barry went up to the sergeant-major to check that they were all going in the same lorry, and when he addressed him as "Sergeant-major" in his accustomed manner, the senior NCO turned to him and said in that strong Scottish dialect which Barry would soon learn to recognise a mile away:-

"While you are here sir, you will address me as "Sir" sir, and I shall address you as "Sir" sir,—but" he added with a twinkle in his eye, "Only one of us will mean it—sir!" Barry understood perfectly and agreed.

Eaton Hall is a lovely place in the Cheshire countryside and all the lectures were to be given in the main building which had been the home of the Duke of Westminster before he made a loan of the whole place to the army—together with most of the furniture and all the stuffed animal heads festooning the walls around the hall and grand staircase. Billets had been erected in the grounds around the hall which were perfectly adequate for the twelve weeks training period of the commissioning course. The cadets would not spend much time in their billets, as the course was action-packed with outside activities which were very positive in introducing them to the history of the British Army, while at the same time training them to use all the forms of weaponry currently being used in action. Within a few days

Barry had learned how to dismantle an automatic Bren gun and then put it together again quickly with his eyes closed.

The assault courses were even more gruelling than he remembered from 4 T.R., and he was soon praising his last unit for preparing him in advance for this course. Those who couldn't make the grade were unceremoniously returned to their unit as "not officer material". No one wanted to experience that disgrace even though it was carried out very tactfully when some unfortunate individual would just be taken away and put onto a train before anyone knew of it.

There were several exercises carried out on training sites in the countryside far away from the Hall where the cadets were gradually introduced to live ammunition. The most elaborate one was "Operation Marathon" which was carried out on a miniature battle field in the Welsh mountains. The exercise took four days and three nights and was carefully planned so that every man knew what was expected of him. Barry fitted in very well and easily completed the exercise which was ordered to do, so he completed his project during the first night of the exercise, and then disappeared to get some sleep in a well chosen nook in the bushes. He dug a deep hole for himself and two colleagues who were happy to follow his lead. When they reported in to the officer in charge of the exercise on the fourth morning they were congratulated for having completed their mission and being in such good form!

On another exercise a few days later, Barry was sheltering from the cold wind behind a stone wall trying to open his sandwich lunch packet with his frozen fingers when an immaculately dressed officer appeared behind him and started to engage him in a friendly conversation about his progress.

"You seem to be doing very well here!" he said, and Barry smiled back at him because he was actually feeling miserable and freezing cold, and all he wanted to do was to get back to the Hall and have a good hot bath. The officer sat down next to him and they made an incongruous couple with Barry looking miserable in his dirty rough denims with webbing pouches all over the place, and his tin helmet askew, and the officer sitting there looking immaculate in his well pressed uniform and highly polished Sam Brown belt.

"Have you thought about signing on?" went on the young captain. Barry was quite thrown by the question, as nothing along those lines had even crossed his mind, so he just shook his head.

"Well you should think about it," said the captain getting into his stride, "You have already done a year in training, and if you sign on for a three year short-service commission, it will only make a total of four years service instead of two, and you would then be on double the pay of a National Service officer, and be given a bonus of five hundred pounds when you come out."

Eaton Hall Officer Cadet School

"Five hundred pounds!" exclaimed Barry. He had never imagined such a large amount, and immediately thought that it would be enough to buy a motor car. "I must think about that. Can I tell you tomorrow?" They left it there but the conversation made Barry start to think about his future. He had been too busy with his training before and had made no plans, but he was no longer sure that he wanted to go on to university, and he had no job to go back to. He had been hoping that his uncle would have offered him a job in his travel company, but he had never mentioned it, or even discussed his future, so he presumed that he was expected to find some new career for himself, and he needed time to think about this. He seemed to be doing well in the army, so why not extend it a bit? Double pay and a bonus of five hundred pounds—wow!

The following day when they were back in the Hall and Barry was coming out of a lecture, the same young officer caught up with him in the corridor and took him to one side.

"Did you think about our conversation yesterday?" he asked amicably.

"Oh yes," Barry replied. "I am quite interested, but three years is quite a long time to be sent to a posting I may not like, which is always on the cards!"

"Do you have any specific ideas for a posting then?" the captain asked.

Barry had been giving the matter considerable thought during the evening, and had discussed the various possibilities with some of his cadet friends in the billet. The fact was that at the time most of them expected to be sent to some unit in West Germany where there were so many British troops to be replaced to do some boring job for the remainder of their service. There would be the usual formal duties and no doubt many military exercises to keep the boys on their toes, but nothing very exciting. On the other hand there were other areas where there was some real active service in many places in the world where usually only the regulars and short service officers were sent to. These included Kenya, where the Mau Mau were making war against the British, then there was Cyprus, where the Turks were fighting the Greeks and the British were trying to control the situation. Then in Korea, where British troops were helping the Americans to fight back the communists, and then Malaya where there were a large number of British troops fighting the communist terrorists in the jungle. That sounded the most promising as it was the farthest posting away from home (which seemed to appeal to Barry for some reason) and it was also the most interesting place to be sent to. No one Barry knew had ever been there, or even to the Far East, so he would try. He turned to the captain and made his point.

"I think I would like to sign on for a short service commission, but only if I can have a posting of my choice," he said.

"Well that is an unusual request," replied the captain, "but if your choice is a reasonable one, I can see what I can do! Where do you have in mind?"

"I was thinking that as I am partially colour-blind and can't be commissioned into my own corps or the infantry, I would like to ask to go into the Ordnance or Service Corps and be attached to a Ghurka regiment in Malaya."

"Well I think that is a very reasonable request," the captain replied, "Just leave it to me and I shall let you know!" and he left Barry feeling that he had made a good positive choice.

A few days later the postings appeared on the notice board in the hallway. There it was! Barry was to be granted a short service commission for three years in the Royal Army Ordnance Corps when he passed out of Eaton Hall, and after a short introductory course at a unit in Aldershot he would be posted to Malaya to be attached to the 99th Ghurka Infantry Brigade in Johore Bahru on the southernmost tip of the country and near to Singapore. Barry was ecstatic about his choice and began looking forward to his new life with great enthusiasm.

The cadets had been going into Chester on a regular basis to enjoy their free time in the evenings, when even the style of their civilian dress was controlled by the regulations of the OCTU. They were obliged to wear only a certain type of gaberdine raincoat and to carry a cane, or "swagger stick" at all times. This was evidently because once they were commissioned and on active service, they would have to get used to carrying it at all times. Anyway they soon got used to it, and Barry was quite embarrassed when one day he was leaving a coffee bar with some of his fellow cadets in Chester—all of them with their canes as usual, so they were quite conspicuous—and he heard a mother sitting in the café say to her young child by way of explanation:-

". . . to beat the dogs off dear!"

Barry made a habit of going into Chester for most of his evenings off duty as there were two good dance-halls in the town, and Blossoms was his favourite where the music was good and there were always some very nice girls who liked to meet the officer cadets and go out with them afterwards. Barry soon formed a relationship with Trudy who was soon letting him take her home after the dance when she always invited him into the living room of her home knowing that her parents were asleep upstairs. Barry had learned about making love from a girl friend he had been seeing at school, so he was a step ahead of his new girl friend—and she did like him to practise on her! Then when it was time for him to go, she lent him her bicycle so that he could return to Eaton Hall and have some sleep before his reveille parade the next morning. The bicycle attracted some interest lying there under his bed, especially during the bed-space inspection by the sergeant-major which was carried out every morning, but they had a good sense of humour and let the matter pass with some sarcastic remark about "having too many wine gums!" as they expected the cadets to use their initiative and enjoy their leisure hours providing it did not interfere with the running of the place.

After some weeks had gone by the cadets were made to feel that their training was coming to an end. Then from time to time they were accosted by representatives of several commercial organisations who wanted to secure their business before they were commissioned and sent overseas. First was a chap sent by Lloyds Bank who was the first to tell Barry that as an officer, his pay would automatically be paid into a bank account, so could he open one for him? Well why not, thought Barry if he was going to have an account, and he chose the branch nearest to his uncle's flat in London.

Then the tailors started badgering the cadets, because they all needed to buy their own uniforms which had to be made with the insignias of their new regiments stitched onto the shoulder tabs for them to wear as soon as they had been commissioned, as most of them had already been given orders as to which unit they were to report to within days after the passing out parade. The new uniform was therefore almost obligatory.

Barry had received orders to report to an Ordnance Officers' Mess in Aldershot for a one week course before going to Liverpool to join the troopship "Empire Clyde", which would take him to Singapore. There he would be met and taken on to the Officers' Mess of the R.A.O.C. attached to the Second Tenth Regiment of the 99th Ghurka Rifle Brigade in Johore Bahru which he soon discovered was a few miles up-country from the causeway which separated Singapore island from the mainland of Malaya.

The passing out parade was even better and smarter than the one at Catterick Camp because it was given much more ceremony in the presence of the families and friends of the cadets who were being commissioned. A very senior army field officer came up from London to take the salute and to make a welcoming speech, and all the cadets were made to feel that they were joining a very elite branch of Society. There was always some prank organised by the cadets for the occasion, and this time some of them had daubed with white paint the sexual organ of the horse under the splendid black statue of Hugh Lupus on the side of the parade ground. It couldn't be missed by any of the spectators and caused great amusement. For the first time in his life Barry's father arranged to come to one of his son's ceremonies, and he came over from Germany and travelled up to watch the parade with

Trudy, but even so Barry felt rather sad for him because his support was being given too late to affect their rather non-existent relationship.

Barry had agreed to meet with some of his cadet friends who also lived in London during their few days leave before they had to report to their next unit. They all wanted to wear their new officers' uniforms in public which they were so proud of having worked for, and the three of them, impeccably dressed in their new uniforms, strolled down Whitehall together to test the reaction from the guardsmen when they walked through Horseguards parade. They picked the time when there would be a changing of the mounted guard, and as they strolled across the yard all the guardsmen in their splendid uniforms were rapidly brought to attention and a salute was given by all of them to the new young officers. They returned the salute in the nonchalant way they had been taught, and were not disappointed by the thrilling experience. It would not be long before they would tire of this when they reported to their new units and salutes would be given to them from all directions. A new life was beginning for each of them.

CHAPTER THREE

"Good day, sir! I am Sidney your batman," said the young man cheerfully as he took Barry's suitcase and put it on the single bed in the smart little room which had been allocated to Barry in the RAOC officers' mess.

"Shall I unpack it, sir?" he went on, and Barry smiled his thanks and appreciation for this rapid initiation into the ways of a new young officer which the more experienced batman fully understood.

"Dinner is at 7pm here sir," he went on helpfully, "and the officers usually gather in the bar at about six thirty for cocktails. They won't be wearing anything formal, so you can go in as you are sir, and I am sure you will meet the colonel. He usually asks one of the junior officers to show you the ropes."

Barry relaxed by reading the literature he had been sent about the Corps he had just joined, and then he checked his itinerary for the next few days which appeared to be action-packed with lectures and briefings in the local vicinity until he returned to London to take the train to Liverpool where his troopship sailed for Singapore a week later.

Once on board the troopship "Empire Clyde" he was shown to his cabin which he was to share with another young officer. He had already been briefed to be a "duty officer" on board the ship, which meant that he had a number of troops to look after. He lost no time in going below decks to check their accommodation. It was quite spacious, but with twenty or more of them slinging their hammocks there, he would not have liked to be sharing with them when they reached tropical climates which they would do when they left the Mediterranean in a few days time to go south through the Suez Canal. He would keep an eye on them to make sure that they were allowed on deck if and when the atmosphere below became too oppressive. In the meanwhile they were all looking forward to the adventure of a posting to the Far East and there was a good atmosphere on board of excitement in anticipation of the voyage to new places.

Barry joined the other officers in the officers' bar, and was pleased to note that most of them were about his age and there were also several members of the opposite sex who were going to join the Queen Alexander's Royal Army Nursing Corps in one or other of the hospitals in Singapore. They were also of about the same age, so there should be some fun on board. The new officers were all going to different units in different destinations, and the conversation was very interesting and the many facilities on board would enable them to keep themselves well occupied for the whole journey.

The first shore leave should have been in Farmagusta on the island of Cyprus, but in view of the hostilities there, the captain decided to anchor well off shore, and they could hear the shells exploding over the island all night and no shore leave was allowed. They took the stores they needed on board by way of landing craft, and then set sail for Port Said not far away. Again they anchored off-shore, but the North Africans are a wily race, and it seemed as though the whole town embarked in small bum-boats to come out to the troopship to try to sell their wares to the troops who were all enthusiastic to buy novel local trinkets. It was only a short stop before they set sail again to proceed down the Suez Canal and into the Red Sea. Now the heat was getting to them all, and they were soon all changing into their tropical gear. Barry had taken some good advice in the officers' mess in Aldershot when an old hand told him not to use up his clothing allowance to buy his tropical clothes until he arrived at his destination where it would be much cheaper and better. He would then make a considerable profit by not needing to spend half the money the army had given for this purpose—and hopefully he would then have enough cash in the bank to buy his fist motor car. All the new young officers wore quite scruffy uniforms for the sea journey and changed into bathing suits for most of the day while they lounged on deck. Then most of them had respectable clothes to wear for dinner in the evening.

On board they lay in the sun and played games on deck for most of the day and flirted with the nurses at every opportunity, and then there were occasional duties to attend to the troops and check that they were keeping their quarters clean and tidy. It all worked like clockwork and they mostly looked forward to the next shore leave which would be in Calcutta and Colombo. It was all new to them all and they compared notes avidly with regard to their various experiences and adventures and took many photographs.

It was not until the ship was safely in its berth in the docks of Singapore harbour that they saw for the first time how tropical uniforms should look. The officers from local units who had been sent to meet them were impeccably dressed in their well-starched and pressed tropical uniforms. They laughed at the scruffy appearance of the new young pallid officers who had come to join them from England, but quickly put them at their ease by assuring them that new uniforms would be made up for them within a very short time in line with the local traditions and dress codes. There was a more serious aspect to their arrival however, as Barry was quickly informed by the army captain who had been sent to meet him, that there was a demonstration outside the Chinese University which was located on their route back to Malaya, and they could expect trouble while passing it. He calmly handed a loaded revolver to Barry and asked him whether he knew how to use it. Barry nodded positively, but wasn't sure how he would react if and when they did meet any trouble. He had become quite a good shot at Eaton Hall and was proud of his marksmanship. This would be his first experience of shooting at real people though, so he was quite nervous.

They saw the hundreds of swarming students around the university building long before they got there. They were driving up the wide Bukit Tima dual carriageway with a huge deep drain in the middle of it to deal with the flood waters in the monsoon season. The students saw the small topless military jeep coming up the road towards them from Singapore city with only two officers in it, and thought they would make some kind of demonstration around them. A few of them broke away from the crowd and started running towards the road waving their arms and clearly intending to reach the oncoming jeep. Captain Jack had other ideas, and as soon as one of the students climbed out of the monsoon drain clearly intending to impede them, he fired his revolver at the road in front of him which brought the student to a quick stop and change of plan. Barry followed suit, and so by firing only about three rounds each into the monsoon drain, all the students who had thought of making trouble ran back again to join their friends on the campus to keep their skins in one piece. Barry heaved a sigh of relief and wondered what he was letting himself in for.

They drove across the long causeway which joined Singapore Island to the mainland of Malaya and Barry listened to Captain Jack's lurid description of how an entire company of the Argyll and Sutherland Scottish Regiment had been wiped out there by the Japanese in the war a few years before when they tried to oppose the Japanese conquest of Malaya and Singapore by charging over the causeway in 1942. It was a very different matter now, and the British were again firmly in charge of the country, to the extent that very few military vehicles were even checked when they went through the customs barrier and Captain Jack's jeep was just waved through and past all the civilian motor cars which were queuing up to be searched by the customs officials.

They drove up the drive to the officers' mess and Barry was quickly introduced to the number one boy who immediately shouted for Choy. This was the Chinese boy who had been allocated to be the private servant to Barry from now on, and who took his bags and carried them through the mess and down to a grass hut just behind the main building. This was apparently where all the new officers began their occupation of the mess, and as senior officers were posted away and left, then the remaining officers all moved their rooms up to those of a better standard. Barry was thrilled with the new tropical environment, but he was slightly concerned by the large number of different insects which seemed to inhabit his room without any opposition, and when he asked Choy about this, the boy laughed and indicated that no room was safe or healthy without its share of small lizards to feed off the mosquitoes and other small insects which would otherwise be a greater danger and nuisance. Barry was pleased to see that the bed was a decent size and that it had a huge mosquito net stretched around it on a steel frame. The walls of the room were made of strong grass reeds woven between long poles, so although the room was weather proof, it was not at all sound-proof and the noise made by the millions of crickets in the wild jungle bush backing onto the mess garden was deafening. He would just have to get used to that.

Choy sorted out Barry's clothes and told him which ones he should keep in his damp proof metal trunk which Barry had been well advised to buy in England (with his full name and address of his posting in Malaya and to have it shipped over) to keep his delicate possessions and leather items in to stop them going mouldy, which was a serious hazard in that tropical heat and extreme humidity. Choy then arranged for the local tailor to come in and measure Barry up for all the different uniforms he would need. The "number one" blue uniform he had been persuaded to have made by the enthusiastic tailors at Eaton Hall was destined for the scrap heap after only having worn it for one evening at the first Ordnance Corps officers' mess. The new tropical uniforms were quite different, as the uniforms worn during the day were a smart dark green heavily starched cotton, with short trousers which would be changed at least twice a day and then washed and starched by Choy. The dress uniform with long white trousers was made of brilliant white starched cotton and would be worn only when he was duty officer or on special formal parades and that was worn with a Sam Brown belt and a highly polished sword in a scabbard. The usual evening wear was a short white jacket which was worn over a white shirt with a black bow tie. That went with blue trousers with a red stripe down the side and cummerbund around the waist.

Everyone in the mess was kind and welcoming even though they tried to shock and scare the newcomers with various stories of local horrors usually about dangerous insects and animals in the area. It seemed that only snakes were a real danger as the mess was situated so close to the jungle "bush" but apparently they could easily be avoided. Malaria was rife in that climate, but providing everyone took their Paludrin tablet every morning there was no danger there, even though mosquito bites were never pleasant and always seemed to be aimed at the new boys much more than the old lags. Salt tablets were also taken every day to replace the salt lost through the skin by heavy perspiration.

The Colonel was charming and put Barry at his ease immediately by making him feel welcome and part of the unit. There was a strong discipline of seniority in the mess where some of the captains never spoke to junior second-lieutenants, but this was counteracted by many of the older senior majors being more jovial and friendly, as among other things, they needed the assistance of younger partners to help them win snooker matches which were played in the mess every evening. They also wanted to tell all their old yarns to someone about their days in the war, which were usually exaggerated but nevertheless entertaining for the first few times of hearing them. Barry enjoyed learning about old military traditions in the same way as he had enjoyed keeping up traditions so avidly at his boarding school, so he was keen to learn how to do the right thing, and he quickly fitted in with his new mess life.

On his first morning the colonel sent for him and told him that he would be working for Major Thompson who was in charge of ensuring the efficient supply of armed vehicles to the troops further "up-country". Armoured vehicles were of no use for active jungle warfare which was being fought locally against the communist terrorists, but they were crucial for keeping up regular supplies to the troops nearby at various strategic points. He was given an office to share with Bill Thompson who was a regular officer and therefore had quite a different attitude to his career from those who were either doing their National Service, or who had signed on for short-term engagements like Barry. He looked forward to the day when the army would again only be for the regulars and therefore be more professional than at present. He was a good sort though, and taught Barry many useful things about the army and about the jobs in hand.

Bill was a married man of forty four and he lived with his wife and daughter who had just finished school in Singapore. They had married quarters not far away from the unit, and soon Barry was invited to dinner and met Jackie their daughter whom he fell for immediately as she was lovely. He wasted no time and immediately asked her to go out with him as all his evenings were free except for the occasional days when he was duty officer. Jackie was eighteen now and a real beauty with her long blonde hair, and she liked to dress well and to go out with Barry to dinner in one of the many Indian or Chinese restaurants in Singapore, or even better when they went to one of the many lovely hotels on the beach where they played live dance music and the atmosphere was so romantic. They both loved ballroom dancing and they were good at it and could dance all evening in each other's arms.

There was no control over their free time which was plentiful, and both of them were enjoying their first real freedom, so they were not at all restrained or shy, and after a good night out they would stop the car by some stretch of completely deserted beach and strip off their clothes to swim in the warm sea waters of the Singapore Straits. They dried each other off in the pleasantly cool night air before making passionate love on the soft golden sand without any fear of being seen or interrupted. The beaches were always deserted after dark and life was wonderful for them both.

Barry enjoyed his job as he was given his own topless jeep to drive around the huge depot to check on the progress of all manner of supplies which had been requested by the British army units positioned throughout the region. They were everywhere in the jungle and were tracking down the last few communist terrorists hiding out there. They needed to be constantly supplied with stores, and Barry's unit looked after them by sending to them all the supplies, arms and ammunition that they needed as quickly as possible, and looked after everything for them with the exception of their food which was provided by the Catering Corps. Communist terrorists were still causing trouble on the roads, and also from time to time to the civil population in their villages which were located off the main roads.

The supply line back to G.H.Q. in Singapore was very efficient, but sometimes something would get stuck in the supply line and Barry's job was to track this down and make sure that the goods were released as soon as possible to the troops in the front line and he always kept them notified of what was happening. He soon became known as "the Chaser" which he knew had more meanings than one after his earlier exploits with some of the officers' daughters, but he took it in good spirit as it was well meant, and every time someone saw the Chaser's jeep driving into their part of the base, they knew they had better have an answer to his queries about some delay or another, as this would be reported to the colonel and to the C.O. of the unit concerned.

After a few months the whole supply base including Barry's unit was moved further up-country to Kota Tingi to keep up with the troops they were supplying in their military action against the communist terrorists. They were being driven further up the peninsular away from Singapore and all points of civilisation. They were losing their grip and were gradually being driven up further into the northern jungles, and there were fewer and fewer of them as the local people no longer saw any point in assisting them. They had just become a nuisance and their political point had been lost and abandoned. Barry's officers' mess was moved to a jungle location, but he had bought a good motor car, so he didn't mind driving down the road that little bit further to pick up his Jackie and take her out for the evening as usual. There was supposed to be a curfew and all cars were stopped at various checkpoints after sunset and sent home, but Barry's nocturnal trips were soon recognised by all the guards at the various checkpoints along the way who just waved him through. Young officers got away with anything.

Barry's favourite night spot was Raffles Hotel which was in the centre of Singapore near Collier Quay. The old hotel had a famous bar and restaurant with a superb dance band. Evening dress was compulsory which Barry and Jackie both enjoyed wearing, and the place was never crowded, so they could dance to their hearts' content. Barry was amused to see that the other ranks seemed to enjoy watching them through the open windows from the top of the wall of the NAAFI canteen which was on the opposite side of the road from the hotel, and he often wondered about the strange class distinction which created the barrier between them. There was nothing to prevent a corporal, or even a private soldier from dressing up and coming into the hotel to enjoy an evening in the same way as he did, but somehow and for some reason best known to themselves, this never happened. NCOs and private soldiers went out to bars and clubs in their tropical uniforms; officers and their ladies went out in evening dress to other officers' messes or to hotels and restaurants.

All good things had to come to an end and Jackie's father was eventually posted back to England. The whole family went back with him so Barry was left without his Jackie and he knew he would miss her. Not for long though, because there were always other officers with daughters, and it was not be long before he was introduced to another officer's lovely daughter.

All the officers in the mess seemed to be characters of different sorts, some of whom were entertaining and others were just bores who seemed to enjoy giving trouble to the junior officers. Charles was a captain in the Ordnance Corps who was also a short service officer, which he had kept renewing as he didn't know what else to do if he left the army. He was very cynical about women, so he was the complete opposite to Barry and used to go out of his way to annoy him whenever the subject arose. That would be quite frequently, because Barry often found himself in Charles's office who was teaching him the technique of using different golf clubs for propelling golf balls across the floor into a waste paper basket. He talked a lot about local politics and taught Barry many things about the problems in the Far East and what would probably happen to most of the other smaller countries nearby within a year or two of Malaya and Singapore attaining their independence. Then one day Charles wasn't there any more, and the story soon got around that he had been sent home because he was getting a divorce from the wife he had left at home, and the regiment would not allow their officers to divorce. So he was ordered to go home and no one knew what would happen to him there—presumably he would serve out his time at the regimental headquarters in Didcot and then be discharged. No one gave it a second thought as everyone moved on sooner or later, but it was just odd that he hadn't said goodbye to anyone and they all thought this fitted in with his caustic personality. He had never had any close friends there.

Peter was another ageing captain who was serving out his posting with the regiment, but he was the opposite to Charles, because he had left his wife at home and chosen to serve out his commission in the officers' mess while saving up his pay to take home to his wife when he would leave the service and retire with her somewhere in the English countryside. He seemed to be having a miserable existence as he never enjoyed any of the evenings out in the town with his fellow officers. Eventually he decided that he would take just one holiday before he left the Far East, and he arranged to go to Hong Kong and stay at an officers' mess there to economise and see some of his old army mates who were stationed there.

He never came back though, as on the last evening of his holiday Peter agreed very much against his better judgment to go out for a drunken spree with his friends into Kowloon. Then on the way back to the Mess after they had visited many of the favourite haunts and drunk too much late into the night, the officer who was driving the jeep and was also very drunk, had driven the vehicle straight into a wall at a very high speed and killed them all. So Peter never enjoyed all the money he had gone to such pains to save, but presumably his widow had at least benefited financially from his sacrifice and his pains.

Barry spent most of his leisure hours with the younger officers in the mess, and if they had no other plans, they would drive into Singapore together and visit one of the many fun spots on the island. "Happy World" was one of the favourites where there were the usual fairground attractions during the day for children, but later in the evening there was a good dance-hall which was open late into the night. A large number of attractive young "taxi-dancers" worked there, who charged a fixed price for each dance, and single men would buy tickets at the door and use them to dance with any girl of his choice. He would then usually end the evening by taking one of the girls home to her grass hut in some local village kampong and having sex with her for a small additional fee.

If the young officers didn't go out to one of the regular fun spots, then they would usually make up a small party to go out to dinner in Singapore, which was usually to a good Indian or Chinese restaurant in Bugis Street or other places in the centre of the lively town. This became a famous area for other things as well, as both female and male prostitutes would gather there in full view of all the diners. Barry didn't take any chances that way, but he was pleasantly surprised that none of his friends picked up any diseases, as so many risks were being taken, and the streets were filthy. On one occasion while sitting at a balcony table in a reputable Chinese restaurant waiting for his meal to be cooked and served he looked down and watched a cook immediately below him openly wash himself in the same kwali which he was about to cook the meal in for some of the customers. It all seemed to be perfectly normal and accepted practise. Perhaps they had all become immune to the bugs which must have thrived in the area. The large rats were always in full view scurrying up and down the open drains down the side of all the small streets.

Months went by and Barry was earning enough money to start travelling to some parts of the Far East which his colleagues were telling him about. First he travelled up the whole of the Malayan peninsular to see both the Eastern and Western coastlines of the large peninsular and to visit the places of particular interest in the middle, like Kuala Lumpur, Penang and the Cameron Highlands. All of this was made much easier for him by the army who actually paid for officers to go to the Cameron Highlands after a year in the humid tropical atmosphere of the tropical climate as it was supposed to be good for them as a "change of air" station. It was much cooler and peaceful up there in the hills in the north of Malaya and very relaxing. The communist terrorists did the same thing, and in the same region, but there were never any incidents up in the hills, and it felt as though both sides had agreed that it was to be considered as neutral territory.

There were no single girls up there, and Barry would have found it all very boring, but for the first time he was attracted to a Chinese girl who worked in the house where a group of British officers were staying with their wives, and when the married couples went out to play golf or walk around the picturesque landscape, Barry would be entertained by the lovely young Chinese girl who was always smiling at him and enjoyed sitting on his lap and letting him play with her slim smooth body. The she would drag him into his bedroom and take off all his clothes and giggle at him while she taught him some Chinese tricks.

Malaya is a big country so it suited Barry to combine his change of air holiday with visits to other parts of the colony, so he decided to visit a few other British Officers' messes where in the best British tradition he was made to feel welcome and he paid nothing for the privilege. He also received many surprises by bumping into old cadet colleagues who had been posted there after they had lost touch with each other after the hectic days of Eaton Hall and their separation after the passing-out parade. He bumped into his old chum Sam in one of the officers' messes who took him to see places near his unit, like Port Dickson and Serumban and islands off the Eastern coast which were very beautiful. He was never shot at during his long drives in his little car, and knew that the political problems would soon come to an end. Then they would all go home.

Barry enjoyed being a platoon officer in charge of his men who were mainly Malay boys under him, and they constituted most of the supply troops and looked after the garrison and all its supply needs for the active troops in the jungle who were mainly Ghurkas from Nepal. The discipline was good and the respect they showed to the officers was second to none which made Barry's job that much easier. On the other hand it worried him that he never received any complaints about anything from his men which he thought was too good to be true, particularly with regard to the food, so he mentioned it to the colonel one day.

"Anyway, how would I know whether any complaint about the food was genuine or not?" he asked him. "I mean they are always given their own type of hot spicy food which we know very little about!"

"Quite right, my boy, and well done!" was the colonel's reply. "You have just volunteered for a cook's course!" and walked away with a smile. He knew from his long experience in the army that there would never be any complaints about the food from the men, because the cook-sergeant and the duty-sergeant between them would deal with any possible complaint long before it got to the ears of the duty officer. He also knew that the standard of the food provided to the men was very good, but nevertheless it would be a good idea to have a young officer in the battalion who had been on a cooking course and could speak to the catering staff in their own language and possibly help them in case of any problems with the rations from GHQ. He would also be very useful in the officers' mess for keeping an eye on the cook-staff there.

There seem to be courses for everything in the army, and always staffed by experts, so when Barry was sent off for his four week course to the Catering Corps training course for officers at Nee Soon Garrison on the northern side of Singapore Island, he learnt a lot about cooking from professional cooks in a very short time. This was to stand him in good stead for many years and enable him to appreciate many aspects of the science and art of cooking for all his life. The classes started with lessons which taught him the basic ingredients of all good cooking, and then went on to examine the origin of different meats and vegetables and how to prepare them, and then to the intricacies of blending eastern spices to produce the exotic curry dishes from that part of the world.

At last he knew which parts of the animal certain cuts of meat came from, and why fillet steak was so tender and needed very little cooking, and why brisket and loin were that much tougher and could therefore cook for so much longer without disintegrating and were therefore so much better to put into a curry dish which was usually cooked for a long time to assimilate the spices. Preparing the spices was a novelty for the young English officers on the course who had never come across them in the raw, and they were soon identifying coriander and cumin seeds by their strong aromas and learning to grind them with fresh chillies with a pistle and mortar before frying them with variations of other spices to release their strong blended aroma into the meat to be cooked. The rice was never really clean, so it was washed usually four or five times until the water was no longer milky and the grains were shiny. Then the rice was always boiled with exactly one and a half times its volume of clean water and when this was all soaked up, it was left to stand to dry out, when the perfectly cooked dry rice was served and literally poured out of the huge vat it had been cooked in. Back in the regimental cookhouse this procedure was followed twice every day for the men, so it was vital that the officers in charge should know what was being done and why.

Army days in Malaya

Traditional dress of Malay States

A Gurkha wife in the barracks

Malay children at home   Young Malay Taxi dancer

The colonel knew what he was doing, and when Barry returned from the course he was immediately given the position of messing officer for the officers' mess so that he could use his newly acquired knowledge and liaise with the Number One Boy and the mess cook every day to ensure that they produced the best meals possible for his brother officers. The favourite meal of the week was the curry tiffin on Sundays, when several excellent curries were served to chose from. The table was always covered with small dishes or "sambals" which were tasty additions to the different curries like popadums and "hundred year old" eggs and many other delicacies which were all good and elaborate. It became such an occasion that many of the married officers made excuses to have lunch in the mess away from their families on that day and make a bit of a party of it which went on late into the afternoon before everyone retired for a long siesta.

The habit of automatically giving responsible jobs to the youngest officers did not always pay off, and one day the colonel asked one of the junior officers to take charge of the arrangements for an evening tennis tournament in the grounds of the officers' mess to which he had invited the married officers and their wives. The young officer who was detailed to prepare the equipment for the event discussed the details of all the necessary arrangements with the Number One Boy who always gave the impression that he had understood everything, and usually he had as he was very competent, but on this occasion he knew nothing about the huge generator which the colonel had commandeered from the unit to provide outside lighting for the tournament. Neither did the young officer who simply switched on the huge engine and then disappeared to go out on the town for his own evening date. When he returned to the mess later expecting to find the evening in full swing with a bar full of happy tennis players, he was surprised to find an empty mess with everyone having retired to bed or gone home to their married quarters.

In the morning no one spoke to him at breakfast except for one friendly soul who told him that the colonel would probably have something to say to him. No sooner had he arrived at his office than the colonel sent for him and told the sad story of how all the families had arrived at the mess the previous evening expecting an enjoyable time under the floodlights, when suddenly the generator exploded and put the entire garden area into darkness. The poor young officer was listening to it all standing firmly to attention. Had he not even thought of checking the water and oil levels in the machine before he handed over to the Number One Boy? The poor young man was not so practical and would not have known where to find the apertures for those substances in that huge machine, and no one had thought to tell him. The colonel dismissed him knowing that he himself was primarily to blame for this mistake and the consequences. Then in due course when the broken parts of the huge machine had been retrieved, the REME officer in charge of the recovery made a present to the lad of the brass big-end which had sheared off the piston head out of the engine when it had blown up so dramatically with such unfortunate consequences. It made a good ash tray.

Most of the functions at the officers' mess were run extremely efficiently as the staff were so used to giving them. There was a formal dance of some sort at least once a month for the wives and other guests of the officers of the regiment when everyone attended in full evening dress. This meant short white "monkey jackets" for the officers with all medals, and long evening dresses for the ladies with lots of jewellery. A good live band was always hired from Singapore and the dancing was in the formal ballroom style and enjoyed by all. Then just as regularly there were officers' mess nights for the officers alone which they attended in their best mess kits which again were worn with medals. That was a completely different matter for the men only, and it always degenerated into a drunken session with some ridiculous and sometimes dangerous games played after the dinner and much wine had been consumed. The drunken exploits became more and more flamboyant, and on one occasion when Barry was invited to attend such a mess night in another officers mess where the dining room was on the first floor, he witnessed two subalterns being thrown out of the window (with the settee they were sitting on) to land unceremoniously on the lawn below without any serious injury being caused. The window needed replacing as did the settee, but the officers in the mess were used to paying for such incidents and it was all considered to be a normal part of an officer's life.

The colonel usually had lunch with his officers in the mess every day, and he used the occasion while he was having his coffee to shake a pair of ordinary dice to decide the time in the night when the duty officer for the day would have to turn out the guard. The guard was mounted at 7pm, so if the total of both dice added up to eight or more then it would be a late night surprise turnout for the guard on duty that night, but if the total was between two and seven, then it was an uncomfortable early morning call. Otherwise the duty officer just wandered about the huts of the unit and checking the fences wearing his full white dress uniform with a highly polished Sam Brown belt and a glistening ceremonial sword at his side. He continued to wear this full uniform until he had dismissed the parade of the entire battalion which he inspected in the morning at the beginning of their day and the end of his.

Sometimes in the night the duty officer's telephone would ring and someone would be asking him to go and check on some disturbance, but this was very rare, and it was usually a friendly call inviting the duty officer to pop in somewhere for a drink or a chat on his rounds. Barry did enjoy visiting some of the wives in their family houses inside the perimeter of the camp. They usually invited the duty officer to call in when their husbands were away or out for the evening. Some of them had ulterior motives and others were just being hospitable. The gossip was even more fun than the visits.

As time went by Barry became more adventurous and decided that before his tour of duty and his military service came to an end he would make a tour of the parts of the Far East he hadn't seen, and visit Hong Kong and Japan. He was given this opportunity with the promise of a "demob leave" before he was to be sent home, and which he could take at any time. There were many ways of taking such trips, but Barry decided to travel as a civilian to meet local people and stay with them whenever possible and in local hotels. He therefore picked on a merchant steamer which had advertised that it would be sailing from Burma to Japan with a cargo of jute, and would take on board only about a dozen fee-paying passengers. The ship would pick them up in Singapore, and then go on to Hong Kong for a week and then stop in Japan for a month before returning the same way. This would be ideal for Barry and he booked a passage on it.

In the meanwhile Barry continued with his duties as assistant adjutant for the battalion which meant that among other things, he had to distribute the pay to all the troops in his battalion once a week wherever they were in the area. The army routine for this pay parade entailed each man having his own pay book checked carefully every week by the pay staff and then returned to the soldier by the paying officer every week with the pay he was entitled to. As he was on active service duty he was also given a sealed tin of fifty Senior Service cigarettes.

Barry used to enjoy the trip to the bank in the town together with his driver and one armed guard carrying a Lee Enfield 303 rifle which was loaded with one round of live ammunition. It never really occurred to them that they were such an easy target in that open Land Rover as there had never been any previous incidents of armed robbery. The local military problem was purely a political one, and the communist bandits did not seem to be interested in stealing money or possessions of any sort which would not have been much use to them in their jungle hide-outs. So Barry went into the bank every week with the pay clerk to draw out the money he needed to pay to the troops, and when this had been checked back in the office, the three of them set out again to find all the men in the battalion wherever they were on duty, and to hold miniature pay parades in the jungle and different parts of the encampment.

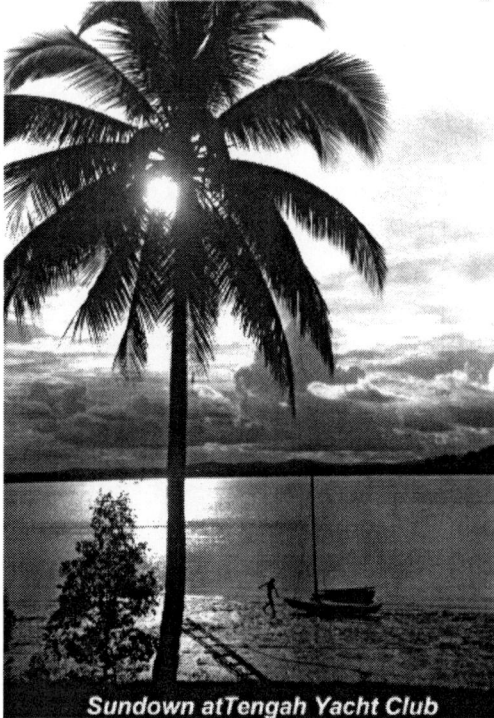

Sundown at Tengah Yacht Club

On each occasion the names of the soldiers were called out by the pay clerk who had been responsible for putting the correct amount of cash into each pay book. The soldier named then marched forward smartly and saluted the officer and took his pay book, money and cigarettes from him. Then he quickly checked the money and stepped back one pace to salute again and say "Pay and paybook correct, sir!"

There was a special unit of pay clerks in the adjutant's office who spent their entire time calculating and checking each man's pay for the next week, so there were never any mistakes with that, but Barry was personally responsible for ordering the correct number of tins of cigarettes from the

General Headquarters, and he found this was getting difficult as there were always men being posted in and out of the battalion, so he made a habit of always ordering a few tins extra so that there would never be a shortfall. After a few months he mentioned the fact to the colonel that he was accumulating these extra tins and he was not sure what to do with them.

"For heaven's sake!" the colonel replied, "You were given that pip on you shoulder on the basis that you had sufficient initiative to work out problems like that for yourself!"

Barry took the hint and put the extra tins to one side which he accumulated in his metal trunk to take home with him in due course. No one wanted to take them from him, so what else could he do with them? He may as well keep them as he would be smoking just as much when he went home, and these extra tins would keep him going for years! No one had mentioned to any of them that cigarettes were dangerous to health, but then no one would do so then, as there were other dangers to life which were much more apparent.

Barry was fascinated by Japan as no one had a good word to say about the people or their country even though it was supposed to be so cultured and have such an interesting history. The fact was that they had made such a bad name for themselves during the war by treating their prisoners so badly, especially in Malaya and Singapore, and then in Burma where so many prisoners had died of malaria or other diseases resulting from malnutrition, or they had been brutally killed by their guards. He knew that he would have a problem with the language as so few people there would speak English and he would not even be able to read any numbers, or street names or menus which would all be in Japanese characters. He therefore had to learn some of the spoken language, and as time was too short for him to learn any of their characters, it could only be done phonetically. Books were not very good for phonetic purposes so he would have to try to find someone who spoke the language. The difficulty was that none of the permanent local staff in the camp would admit to knowing any Japanese or they feared that they would be accused of having been a collaborator with the occupying Japanese troops during the war which was still a bad slur, but eventually he found an old Chinese storeman who didn't worry so much, and who agreed to help him providing that he didn't tell anyone who had helped him. That was a fair deal and didn't cost him anything.

CHAPTER FOUR

The day arrived for Barry to leave for his holiday and he found the M.S. Santhia moored up in the docks without any difficulty and soon made himself at home in the little cabin which had been allocated to him. Then he made his way around the ship to get his bearings and soon found himself meeting the other passengers who were wandering around aimlessly doing the same thing. They were all asked to attend a meeting when they met the captain and several other members of the crew including the Purser who told them all about the ship and how the voyage would be conducted. It all sounded very exciting, and then they were asked to choose the kind of food they would like to have for the whole journey so that the cook would know how many Indian meals and Chinese meals etc., he would need to prepare. Barry quickly decided that as the chef was of Indian origin he would stick to Indian food and so he was allocated to the Indian table. He was pleased to see that other Europeans had made the same choice.

There were two Chinese boys called Wong and Chong on the next Chinese table who were both about Barry's age and they soon all made friends with each other and started to enjoy playing deck games together. Then there was Ulla a young German woman who was travelling alone, and Barry soon met her and struck up a friendship there as well. The only English female passenger was Mary Stockdale who was married to a Brigadier from GHQ in Singapore who had been sent away on a long course leaving her alone, so she had decided to fill in the time of his absence with a holiday cruise. She was much older than Barry but decided to take him under her wing and try to persuade him to stay in the army and to sign on as a regular officer. They had many conversations about it, but Barry had already made up his mind to leave the army when his short service commission expired, even though he still had no idea what he was going to do when he returned to England.

They became quite good friends, and Barry was relieved to find that she was not trying to be flirtatious and so she could become a good friend whom he could confide in about his problems. Unfortunately she was not very helpful as her replies always seemed to lead to her advising him to stay in the army and letting them look after him as clearly the army had always looked after her husband and her family. Barry had no intention of becoming a regular soldier because he knew that he had a wild spirit and that rather than taking him up the ladder, it was more likely to lead to his downfall. In such an organisation he had already discovered that an officer had to be nice to a lot of people he didn't care for, and as a single officer to live with them as well. No, he would find his own way in the commercial world.

He enjoyed the cruise and flirted a little with Ulla, so when they arrived in Hong Kong he had a partner to go and see the sights with. They disembarked there together and found their way to the Star Ferry which took them over to the island from the docks. They looked around the many Chinese shops which were so much better than the ones in Singapore at the time, and then when they started the sight-seeing, their first stop was the lovely hotel overlooking Repulse Bay where they had lunch outside in the beautiful garden before they took the cable car up to the top of the Victoria Peak which overlooks the entire island and over most of the New Territories. There were no tall buildings or skyscrapers then.

They returned to the ship after a good day out and Barry was surprised to find a visitor waiting for him in the bar. He turned out to be a friend of Charles, the officer who had been sent home after his divorce and had joined some ex-military set-up in London. They had asked him for a contact in Hong Kong for them to meet. Charles didn't know anyone on the island, but when he had telephoned one of his old chums in the mess they told him that Barry would be calling into Hong Kong for three days and could be found on the Santhia on any one of those days. Simon was very English and seemed to be quite lost in Hong Kong as he had never been in the Far East before, but his company in London were apparently very worried about the possibility of the Chinese market opening up soon when the cheap products would suddenly be made available to the entire American continent.

Simon warmed to Barry very quickly and was keen that he should set up a meeting for him with a Chinese contact on one of the days Barry would be in Hong Kong again on his return trip from Japan. It all seemed to be a simple matter of tightening up on the contract which the Chinese company had with the British manufacturer. Barry could see immediately that the whole of the British/Chinese market could be seriously endangered when the barriers were opened to the rest of the world through the new American friendship pact which was bound to be signed within the next year. Timing was crucial and Barry promised to help if he could and said he would leave a message for him to follow up when the rendezvous had been arranged with the contact in Hong Kong. Simon gave him his card and said that he should call his London number if he heard nothing upon his return to the island in one month's time. He also gave him the number of an associate in the New Territories to contact if he heard nothing from anyone, and then he passed a sealed envelope to Barry which he said was for him to open when he had left and to keep the contents secret under any circumstances. He was going back to London where he said he felt much more at ease.

Barry looked forward to his new commercial venture which apparently had nothing at all to do with the army or his military position, so he determined not to tell anyone about it until he had spoken to the commercial contact on the return trip. All he could imagine was that the British company wanted to use an in-between man they could trust as he had no position on the island of Hong Kong or with the Chinese authorities and would therefore be completely trustworthy to help with their negotiations. As soon as Simon had taken his leave and was seen scurrying down the gangway to the quay and away into the crowded streets, Barry made his way back to his cabin and opened the envelope. There was a bundle of American dollars inside and a note in a handwriting which he quickly recognised even though he had not seen it for some weeks:-

"Dear Barry,

As you know I could not remain as an officer in the army as a divorced man, and I was going to leave it soon anyway to join this company which is doing very well with its import business with several companies in China. The business is growing quickly but the last thing they need is for the Americans to rob them of their business when the trade barriers are opened.

I hope you don't mind that I have given your name as a likely candidate to be one of our agents as I know that you intend to leave the army soon and will probably be happy to have an opening to move into.

You will be contacted very soon to meet one of the Chinese company directors, and I hope you get on and will co-operate with him to your mutual financial advantage.

I look forward to meeting you again when you return home.

Kind regards and best wishes,
Yours truly,
Charles Keaton"

Barry counted the money and found that he had been given two thousand dollars in hundred dollar bills. He had never been paid so much in his life before and he quickly put it away again and found a very safe place to hide it in his old clothes at the bottom of his travel bag. He thought that would be much better for a young man in his position than by drawing attention to himself by using the ship's safe,

There were many British troops posted around various garrisons on the island and many more up in the New Territories to guard the fence dividing the colony from the Chinese Republic, but of course the political problems were different there from the ones in Malaya and elsewhere in the Far East. Barry decided that he would not visit any of the military bases there as this was a purely civilian trip he was taking, and he had not even brought his uniform to make such calls. It was only necessary for him to carry his officer's identity card with his passport in case he was asked for it.

After a three day stop at the island, they set sail for Japan where they docked in Yokohama. The ship then unloaded its cargo and made its way south down the coast to Kobe where it would commence its journey back to Singapore four weeks later. The passengers had this time to look around the Japanese countryside and make their own way to Kobe in time for the departure date.

Barry teamed up with Wong and Chong to make straight for the centre of Tokyo and check into a small typically Japanese hotel in the Ginza before exploring the night life of the city. They were immediately confronted with the main obstacle for them which was that none of them could read any signs which were all in Japanese characters, so they had no idea of the name of any street, or number of any bus or train. They would have to rely on meeting people who spoke some English or hope that Barry could make himself understood with the little Japanese which he had picked up from his helpful storeman.

They enjoyed the atmosphere of the Ginza with all its noise and bustle, and they couldn't wait to go into a little nightclub to meet some lovely

Japanese girls. The serving girls all spoke a little English and were very open and keen to join them and go with them to their hotel when the place closed for the night. They were not prostitutes and did not ask for any money. They just made friends and were happy to show the boys how to drink hot sake. This was very potent which they soon got used to as it seemed to be served with everything.

Barry fell in love with his bar girl Kazuko on sight as she was paying him so much attention and touching him as she served them with their drinks. She also had a lovely little giggle which seemed to cover her embarrassment at being admired so openly. She was tall for a Japanese girl and had a lovely slim body which Barry couldn't keep away from, and she kept her hand on his arm or his shoulder all the time. He was determined not to let her go and she seemed to like it and soon intimated that she would be staying with him. Eventually they all left together and walked a short distance around the corner to their small well-lit and clean-looking hotel. None of the boys had stayed in a Japanese style hotel before and didn't realise that there would be no furniture in the room except for a cupboard and small table with a delightful flower arrangement. The bed was a rolled-up duvet in the cupboard which they spread out on the floor when they wanted to sleep. They all took their shoes off at the front door when they were immediately given kimonos to wear instead of their western style clothes which they were asked with polite gestures to hang up in the cupboards.

The next step in the procedure was for them all to have a bath in the hotel bathroom, and as soon as they were in their kimonos they were all ushered below into the basement where they found this. It was large enough to take at least ten people and was already full of steaming clean hot water. There were three more lovely young girls waiting for them at the foot of the stairs and each one took hold of one of the boys to one side and indicated that he was to take off his kimono and stand naked at the side of the bath where she then washed him all over. They giggled incessantly at the embarrassment shown by all the boys, while they rubbed them all over with their warm soapy hands. Then they sponged them off with clear hot water and helped them to lower themselves into the very hot bath. That was a lovely feeling and soon all three of them were sinking into the pure luxury of lying in that clean boiling hot water. Kazuko had deliberately waited for him in their room and left him to discover the pleasures of his first Japanese bath.

Barry was not looking forward to sleeping on the floor, but in fact it was very soft and he was very happy spending his first night with Kazuko who had looked after him and his friends very well in the bar. She had drunk a few glasses of sake herself before they left the bar which made her a little unsteady, but it also gave her the little courage she needed to spend her first romantic night with an Englishman. She enjoyed being with him and they made love passionately and Barry soon found that all the rumours he had heard and had his leg pulled about some supposed weird sexual antics of the Japanese were misplaced and unfounded. She was a very soft loving girl who gave him everything she had—body and soul, and she seemed to be in love with him at first sight. Barry didn't mind at all and determined that he would keep her with him for all his short time in Japan and take her on their travels before he had to leave Japan. It didn't seem to matter to her at all that she was walking away from her job. When Barry became concerned about this and mentioned it to her, she just giggled and assured him that there were many such jobs in Tokyo and that she may even find a better one. She had a lovely open attitude and Barry knew that he would enjoy her company as much as her assistance with his travels.

Wong and Chong came to his room the next morning having sent their girls home, and Barry told them that Kazuko would be staying with them and not going back to her job. This suited them all very well as the boys liked her and all agreed that they did need an interpreter and her English was excellent. So she took them around the city which was very different from any other city any of them had known before, with its incredible noise and bustle. The taxis seemed to be in competition with each other and always blew their horns when they were overtaking each other so the noise was deafening. Then there seemed to be a danger of the wheels of their taxis getting into the tram lines and not being able to get out again!

They visited some very artistic coffee bars, where they were soon surrounded by young Japanese students who wanted to know all about life in the West. They had all heard all they wanted to know about America because there had been so many American troops in Japan since the end of the war, but they wanted to know about other places as well—like England and even Singapore which none of them had been to.

Barry soon got into political discussions about what the young students thought of the war and the unpopularity of the Japanese as a result of it. The students seemed to be a little nonplussed by the question, as they had been brought up to believe that their parents had fought hard to win the war and had then died because they lost. They did not understand anything about rules of war or the Geneva Convention. They implied in their conversation a belief that to impose any rules over methods of fighting a war and taking of prisoners was trying to turn a very serious and deadly business into a game of cricket. It was soon apparent that they had been brought up to think in a very different and more brutal way than western civilisations, and that honour and victory in their old culture had always been a matter of life and death and was to some extent still thought about in that way—hence the easy enlistment of the kami-kazi pilots in the war who flew their planes directly at warships to ensure maximum damage even at the cost of their own lives.

There were many fascinating differences in the day-to-day Japanese culture, and Barry was fascinated by the uniforms worn by the school children which were even more military and identical with each other than at the English public schools which he had thought were rigid enough. The restaurants were good but expensive and red meat was almost impossible to find. The average menu was either fresh raw fish prepared and served in many different ways as "sushi," or "tempura" which was another tasty way of cooking fish, but this time fried in batter. Rice was the staple diet and everything was eaten with short pointed chopsticks which were different from the Chinese ones they were used to in Malaya, but they soon got used to them. They couldn't understand anything on the menus of course, but fortunately most restaurants made plastic models of their dishes and put these in the window, so a customer could just point at the one he wanted.

At the hotel a light breakfast was served to them all in their bedrooms before they met up for their excursions, and Barry asked for an egg thinking that it would be served up boiled. He had apparently not made this clear however, so the Japanese waiter believed that he wanted it raw and brought it still in its shell rolling around on a clean plate. Barry realised that the limits of his knowledge of the language had been reached, so he mimicked to the waiter how he wanted his egg fried in a pan, and so it was soon returned to him lightly fried and still liquid on its own on the plate—with the usual short pointed chopsticks! Barry thought about this but soon gave up and decided to swoop up the egg with both chopsticks together and try to find his mouth! Kazuko returned from her bath and heard the story much to her amusement. She then quickly drank her own breakfast choice of natural fruit juice and they joined the boys to go out on the town.

They decided to go on the bus together to the little village of Myanoshita on the side of Lake Hakone opposite the wonderful sight of Mount Fuji pointing up to the sky in full view of their hotel. It was a lovely peaceful place which they all enjoyed after the madness of Tokyo and made a welcome holiday for Kazuko who said that she so rarely had the opportunity to go to the country. After two days there spent walking in the woods and discovering beautiful sights of wild streams and waterfalls they were ready to move on as their time was limited. They decided to take the fast "bullet" train to Kyoto—the old capital city of Japan before it was moved to Tokyo (which was given its name by merely changing the letters around).

Kyoto was quite different from Tokyo as it had managed to keep most of its historical beauty and charm from the old days, and the cafes and restaurants were a pleasure to visit. Barry and Kazuko had become very close lovers now, so the Chinese boys decided to leave them alone and move on independently. They would meet up again in Kobe to embark for their return voyage, but in the meanwhile they were going to engage in a little more girl-chasing which they found easier as a pair of bachelors. Their poor knowledge of the language had become a joke as their features looked much more Japanese than Barry did, but they didn't care and usually found someone who spoke a little English, so they were no longer as daunted as they had been at first.

Barry and Kazuko stayed on in Kyoto as they loved the atmosphere and found their hotel to be very romantic in its own Japanese way. They had got used to the duvet on the soft floor and spent more time there than they did sight-seeing. It was the first full-time love affair Barry had ever enjoyed, as he had always had to fit his girl friends into his military itinerary before, and had never taken a girl friend away on a holiday. This was bliss and he was enjoying it to the full.

The loving couple were well aware that all good things must come to an end, and they planned to spend their last day in Kobe and have a relaxing evening there before Barry had to embark on his steamer again for the return to Singapore. It was all very romantic but sad for them both, and when the time came, Kazuko was on the quay side with many other friends of the passengers and crew of the ship which was about to set sail. They all had rolls of coloured paper streamers in their hands which they were throwing at their friends gathered along the rails of the ship, and as it departed by slowly leaving the quay with hoots being sounded from the ship's horn, the streamers continued to stretch from the ship to the shore until the last one broke away and the ship was on its way.

Barry tried to put Kazuko out of his mind because there was no way they could continue to communicate, as she could not write in English, and Barry could not write in Japanese, and he did not think that he would ever return there. His mind was soon turning to thoughts of going back to England, but that would be in a few weeks time. In the meanwhile he enjoyed the return passage with the same passengers who were busily exchanging stories of their various adventures in Japan for the few weeks they had been there. Wong and Chong had enjoyed their exploits and told Barry several lurid stories of their encounters with various ladies of the night.

Barry teamed up with Ulla again, and all the other passengers became much closer friends on that return voyage. Mary knew that her brigadier husband would be back from his military conference and that he would meet her at the Singapore quay, and she insisted that Barry should come to dinner at their house in the centre of GHQ in Singapore. Barry was flattered by the invitation, but thought nothing would come of it because of the huge difference in their ranks and age.

Barry said nothing about Simon who had been seen drinking with him at the bar on board before they had left Hong Kong on the way out, but the questions became much more intense when they arrived in Hong Kong again and it was drawn to their attention that the Englishman who had come on board had been found murdered in the back alleys of Kowloon on the same night that he had been seen coming on board to meet Barry. The police were soon on board to ask what anyone knew about him, and they homed in on Barry who could only tell them that he had been sent by a mutual friend and that he didn't know any more about him. Yes, he had his card, but the police already knew about that as he was carrying them in his wallet when they found him. It was all a mystery and they didn't deter Barry any further.

A message was waiting for Barry to have breakfast with a Chinese gentleman the following morning in his office on the island opposite the Mandarin Hotel which he thought would be very safe, so as a completely innocent participant in whatever Simon was involved in he agreed to go. After all, that was what he had been paid handsomely to do and he was an officer and a gentleman and always kept his word.

It did not surprise his fellow travellers when Barry missed breakfast the next morning, as many others had also gone ashore early to take advantage of all the hours available to them to explore the fascinating colony. Barry took an early Star Ferry across to the island and walk over to the office building he had been invited to, and he was soon whisked up in the lift to the top floor where he found a very smartly dressed chinaman waiting for his lift doors to open. He introduced himself as Chow Lee and they walked together into a huge boardroom where two places had been set for breakfast and many dishes were already in place and Barry was invited to help himself to anything he liked while his host took his seat making it clear that Barry should sit next to him when he had taken what he wanted on his plate.

It was all very civilised and the Chinaman was saying very little as he was watching every move Barry made. It was evident that he was very much at home in that vast room and probably had meetings like this very frequently, but Barry just felt that he didn't belong to the same world and he wanted to establish some kind of common ground as quickly as possible.

"Did you know Simon well?" he asked pointedly, and Chow Lee shook his head slowly.

"Meet only once and make acquaintance," he replied shortly. "His company know my company and velly angly!" he went on. "I explain that Hong Kong dangerous for some business men, but motive not clear and police ask many questions. You know him?" he aimed at Barry.

"No," Barry replied honestly, "I only met him once when he said that I should hear from you and then meet you. Why should anyone kill him?"

"Possible that they did not want you to meet me, so please be careful. I have your number in Singapore and better that my agent contact you there where there is no danger. Many soldiers look after you !" and he actually smiled showing his awful uneven teeth.

"What can I do to help?" Barry asked determined to bring an end to the intrigue and to find out what he was being set up for. He had been paid handsomely for something and he dearly wanted to find out whether he was letting himself in for something he didn't care for.

"No problem for you!" assured the Chinaman. "British company make contacts in Far East to protect their Chinese market. Good business for many years and not want to go to American companies who not pay good. Bad business coming soon but we keep friends with your good country. You help with messages and take money for us in Singapore. Many ships come there."

Barry was slowly beginning to understand that there would be some in-fighting when the trade barriers were opened up for China and the Western world, but he could not understand why someone would need to go to the lengths of killing one of the messengers. He could be next.

His chums at the officers' mess were all interested in his stories about Japan, as although most of them had taken a holiday to Hong Kong, and even been posted there, none of them had gone on to Japan which was still considered to be unfriendly territory. Barry tried to convince them to the contrary after his pleasant experiences, but most of the prejudices he came up against were very deep rooted as most of the senior officers had known friends who had died or suffered in the war at the hands of Japanese. Barry did not want to tell them how he knew that modern Hong Kong was getting to be just as dangerous in a different way.

A few weeks went by before the colonel sent for him, and while Barry stood there to attention in the CO's office, the colonel read out a letter he had received.

"This seems to be from a professional letter-writer in Tokyo who is writing on behalf of a young lady who says she is pregnant and that you are the father! Do you know anything about it?"

Barry went red with embarrassment and spluttered some kind of reply about having met a girl while he was on holiday there a few weeks before.

"Well that's OK," said the colonel, quite calmly and smiling at him. "Next time you go on holiday just don't leave your address with the ladies you meet!" He tore up the letter and nonchalantly disposed of it in the waste paper basket behind him, but Barry thought differently. He had cared for Kazuko and didn't like to think that he had made things difficult for her. So he brooded a little.

CHAPTER FIVE

Ian was a R.E.M.E. officer in the mess attached to the unit who had become friendly with Barry and sometimes took him flying as he was trying to clock up the hours to get his pilot's licence. So Barry went to the airport with Ian on several occasions and took the opportunity to ask whether any of the planes flew as far as Japan. It appeared that American cargo planes did stop there sometimes to refuel, he was told, and he arranged for the clerk to telephone him when another one was coming in so that he could try to hitch a lift.

A few days later he received a call from the friendly clerk telling him that an American plane was coming in from Korea the next morning for refuelling before going on to Okinawa, which Barry knew was one of the small islands off the mainland of Japan and would have regular ferry boats going to Yokohama. So the next morning after a quick word with the colonel to excuse himself for dashing off at such short notice, he dashed down to Selangor airport in his officer's uniform and met the American pilot who said that he would be happy to take him along in his large plane as cargo—as long as he didn't try to make it formal or tell anyone. Barry agreed, but unfortunately the American had failed to tell Barry that the plane would be making an overnight stop in Taipeh, the capital of Taiwan which considered itself to be the last remaining bastion of the Chinese Democratic Republic. The problem with that political situation was that the attitude of the British Government towards China differed slightly from the stance of the American government which was so anti-communist that it had never officially recognised the existence of communist China. Britain did, and the Chinese Democratic government in Taipeh did not appreciate that, and as a result did not welcome British visitors. A visiting British officer in full uniform would be most unwelcome as Barry was soon to discover. No sooner had the plane landed and his American pilot invited him to stay with him in the American officers' mess in Taipeh, when a group of angry looking Chinese police appeared on the runway and took Barry with an armed guard to the Grand Hotel in the city. This seemed to be their alternative to taking him to the police cells as they didn't want to go through all the arresting procedures as they knew from the pilot that he would be leaving the city first thing in the morning and taking Barry with him. In the meanwhile he should be kept under lock and key and in true Chinese fashion was given an excellent meal in the hotel. Barry could not have done better and the American pilot was very jealous when he returned in the morning.

They landed safely at Okinawa where Barry thanked his American pilot and soon made his way to the Yokohama ferry. He wasn't sure where he would go from there, but he remembered the way to Tokyo, and everyone was so kind to him when they recognised the British army officer's uniform which had been pressed for him in the Grand Hotel in Taipeh. He soon found his way to the Ginza and the bar where had first met Kazuko. He caused quite a stir walking into the place as they were not accustomed to seeing Englishmen there in uniform, but he was pleased to recognise one of the girls he had met with Kazuko who was still working there. She told Barry that she had seen Kazuko recently who had gone to live with her mother outside the city to have her baby. It appeared that she was very well and happy with her baby boy, and did not expect any help from Barry and had only had the letter written to him out of courtesy. Nevertheless Barry left some money for her with a note of good wishes which he was assured would be translated and passed to her and also his address in spite of what his colonel had told him, in case she wanted to contact him at any time. He could not stay to see her because he had to return to his unit, but he was pleased that he had come to check up on the situation and to make sure that the end of his love-affair with Kazuko would not be the same as in Puccini's opera of Madam Butterfly. He left messages to say that he hoped that Kazuko was happy with her new life as he knew that so many Japanese women were happy with their lives as sole parents, and there was little that he could do to help her. She had said that she did not want to be paid any money, as she believed that the absentee father usually turned out to be unreliable, and anyway she would be well looked after financially by the State.

Barry had decided to make his way back to Singapore via Hong Kong to fit in a visit to Chong Lee whom he would convince that he was coming there expressly for that purpose. The American Air force had been so kind to him before, and for some reason felt responsible for him being held prisoner in the Grand Hotel in Taipeh on the previous trip so they were very helpful and got him onto the flight he wanted into Hong Kong and then on to Singapore the next day. He had told them that he just considered the previous embarrassment in Taipeh to be another adventure, but they wouldn't have it, and they treated him like a hero who had escaped from some terrible prison.

He was soon being greeted by Chong Lee in his grand office in Hong Kong, and as Barry expected he gave nothing away except to indicate vaguely that he had heard that the police were investigating Peter's murder and getting nowhere. They would soon write it off as another small time robbery for money. There were many of those, but not so many of Europeans. The Chinese trade connections with the United Kingdom were still being kept a close secret Chong Lee assured him, and a few changes had been made to the executive staff on the commercial side of his organisation. Contacts had been made by them with outside dealers who were looking at the new marketing prospects for Communist China when it was fully recognised by the outside world. The Chinese mafia operated in a different way to British businessmen, and Barry was horrified to hear that those members of the Chinese staff who had been suspected of infidelity to their Noble Houses had just disappeared and were not heard of again. The story was often told that they had just chosen to return to their families over the border, but no one ever knew that for sure.

The story about Barry's amusing experience in Taipeh in the hands of the Chinese airport police had got back to Singapore, and a few days after his return, he received a telephone call from Mary the brigadier's wife at GHQ to ask him to go and have dinner with her and the brigadier and to tell them about his experience. No one knew anything about his new commercial role as Charles had not let anyone else know. That would have been too dangerous especially after Simon's murder, even though news of that had not been noticed in Singapore.

Barry wore his lightweight Irish linen white suit for Mary's dinner as she had said that it was not to be a formal military dinner, but more of a family gathering. Nevertheless she had invited a few top brass officers who were friends of her husband and who came in full uniform. Barry felt more at ease in his suit as he was beginning to feel that he was on his way out of the army, and he no longer had that fear of authority which he had felt for the first years in the service, and the strict discipline which had been instilled into him and lasted throughout his service. He would have felt very inferior wearing his subaltern's uniform in that exalted company.

The senior officers around him at the dinner party were all much older than Barry and were very jovial over cocktails before the dinner. They continued to exchange amusing stories which Barry thought put his exploits to shame, but they didn't think so, and congratulated him on handling the Taipeh matter so well and keeping a low profile on the incident. On reflection, Barry had to agree that it could have been used against the British government in a very embarrassing way, but the fact was that it wasn't. Also he to admit that he had really enjoyed that Chinese meal on his own in the Grand Hotel in Taipeh. Some years later when he was asked many a time to tell the same story and to explain the cultural differences he found between the Chinese and the Japanese people, he thought that if the Japanese had locked him up with a good meal like that in a top hotel they would probably have sent him a geisha girl as well. Others with bad memories of the war years thought the Japanese would have had him shot—or worse.

There was no mention during the evening of the episode in Hong Kong as no one at the table knew of his association with Simon (which some of them had read about) or even Charles, and those who had known Charles, thought he was a sad character to bring the Regiment into disrepute with his divorce. How little they knew! The world markets around them were about to explode with the admission of China onto the world of commerce, and none of these top brass military toffs seemed to know or care anything about it. They all spoke as though they were more concerned about the few remaining communist bandits hiding out in the jungles of north Malaya and soon to disappear into Thailand. The Emergency was over and all they were all thinking about was their next posting and the short time remaining before they were out of the service and living on their pension.

Barry was made to feel like a young new hero whom they were all glad to meet but he was not so sure, as he felt that in such exalted company there must be at least one or two of those senior British officers who had been briefed to keep an eye open on the changing commercial world which was within their area of military operations. None of them were giving anything away, and all of them chatted jovially enough, but any of them could have been waiting for Barry to give something away. He just had no way of knowing which of them was watching out for him.

The dinner came to an end and they all made their formal farewells and thanked the brigadier and his wife for their hospitality, and made passing jokes to Barry about keeping clear of any civilian Chinese communists he may meet.

Colonel Stockdale was one of the last to leave, and as he shook hands with Barry he said almost inaudibly so that none of the other guests could hear him:-

"Would you like to come to dinner at my place next week? I think there are a few things we could discuss."

Barry promptly accepted with some astonishment as they had hardly spoken during the evening, whereupon the Colonel passed him a card with his full name and address printed on it, and just added,

"Next Thursday then? Eight pm and informal as there will only be us and the wife."

Barry was taken completely by surprise as he had hardly spoken to him during the evening, and all he knew was that he was a very senior colonel who had only recently been posted out from London to command the REME unit at GHQ. He said he would send a car for Barry at the appropriate time and then bade him goodnight as he said that he looked forward to seeing him next week and hearing more about his adventures and travels which they had only brushed over that evening.

The following Thursday the car arrived to collect Barry at 7.30pm and he was driven in silence to his strange and unexpected rendezvous. Colonel Stockdale had been given one of those lovely houses in Selangor, the posh military area of Singapore, with a lavish garden and surrounding walls, and there must have been at least four servants looking after him and his wife. He discovered that they lived alone as they had left their children at boarding schools in England. Jane was one of those charming middle-aged wives who was clearly happy with her lot and seemed prepared to do anything for her husband and his friends as she talked about them a lot. She created a very hospitable atmosphere and welcomed Barry like an old friend even though they had never met before. Soon the three of them were sitting comfortably outside on the veranda to catch some of the evening breeze and enjoying their pre-dinner cocktails. Jane laughed easily and made Barry feel very much at home exchanging stories with him and appearing to be interested in comparing his life as a subaltern with those far gone days when her husband had also been a young lad in the army in Germany. Soon she disappeared to help the staff with the final preparations for the meal and the colonel turned to Barry very seriously.

"Charles should never have got you mixed up with all this commercial stuff. You can see how dangerous it is, but I liked the way you handled yourself at the Brigadier's dinner. Do you think you can cope with it all, or does it worry you?"

"Oh I'm OK, sir," Barry replied, feeling quite relieved to know that at last he had been contacted by someone with authority who was involved in what was clearly a serious and heavy matter which he had been told very little about.

"We don't have passwords or anything like that, you know," the friendly colonel continued, "but Charles had to contact someone here beyond suspicion to carry on what he had to leave behind, and I understand that your meeting with Chow Lee went off well in Hong Kong?"

"Oh yes, sir, but he didn't tell me much, so perhaps you could fill me in?"

"No, I won't do that as it would put you into possible danger, but I shall be asking you to visit certain industrial businesses on the island and even perhaps a rubber plantation or two on the pretext of looking for possible openings for yourself after your commission comes to an end. It is true that you only have about two months left to serve?"

"Yes, that's true, but I think I should like to go home when the time comes!" he answered emphatically, as he was getting tired of the hot damp tropical climate.

"Oh don't worry about that, my boy!" replied the colonel with a friendly smile, "We are only taking advantage of you for a short time to convey some messages and goodwill between some very important business people here. It's just as important for us that you do not become too involved in what they do. Our time is over here, you see, and we don't just want to be kicked out of the back door like the French were in Vietnam and the Germans in Africa. I can tell you that Peter was the director of one of the larger UK companies doing business over here, and apparently he knew too much about Chinese politics for his own good and they didn't like him. He was an accident waiting to happen, so we weren't surprised when they got him. You wouldn't have known it, but he had given away some details of important contracts other companies have here. We soon found out and we don't want any more of that kind of violence, so we are keeping a tight ship from now on with our communications between the important people. Believe it or not your little contribution towards this is very valuable to us without you even knowing it!"

Barry said nothing for a moment as he was not even sure what he had contributed, then he turned to the colonel,

"I suppose that we should be careful about not losing our trading partners here to other parts of the world when the Americans eventually start to recognise communist China and agree to buy their products?"

"So you have seen the danger then!" the colonel smiled back at him for making his life a bit easier.

"The Chinese are actually very loyal people by nature, but they are also very astute business people, so we must make sure that we convince them that their business with the UK is secure and growing. They must feel that there is no need for the ones who are already with us to go looking for more trade or even worse, to move it elsewhere like to our friends across the Atlantic. We know that, but unfortunately we have to deal with underground forces who can see that there are huge profits to be made by diverting cheaply manufactured goods to the new markets."

Barry had the picture clearly in his mind, and could see that he was merely a small part of the large picture in a rapidly changing world where some forces may be at work to try to divert a number of lucrative trades presently carried on with the UK by moving them to American or international companies elsewhere. So this was a goodwill mission he was on as he saw it, and thought he would probably enjoy it.

There were many tough old English planters up country who had run the Malacca rubber plantation since the Second World War with the assistance of very loyal staff to him, but there were murmurings about changes which were bound to take place after the Emergency was over and independence was declared for the new Malaysia. The time had now come, and many of the ambitious local managers could see their opportunity to move in and take control over all the businesses which had always been run by the British before. New laws would soon come in to take away their superiority and some said that they would even be banned from having directorships in local businesses, so the new local managers would be able to take over, and open up new markets with other countries. It could spell disaster for British businesses and trades which had been so carefully built up in the colony like the rubber industry.

There were virtually no Americans in the colony during the time of the Emergency as they had not been asked to assist with the jungle warfare, and they had kept to their own wars in Vietnam and Korea, while the British looked after its own colonies with the assistance only of other members of the Commonwealth like Australia and New Zealand. Independence was going to bring in a lot of trouble though, and the senior military officers were being asked by Whitehall back at home to assist in assuring that there were no huge leakages of commercial enterprises to other countries to the detriment of the local British economy. It was an almost impossible task, and was hardly helped by ambitious politicians who just couldn't wait for the British to leave their country so that they could take over and make their personal fortunes by selling the produce of the local trades to any other country who may be interested.

Barry was asked to go and visit the managers of some of the well-known companies and to be introduced to the aspiring new local managers in the hope of getting the names of foreign companies who may be interested in doing business with the new country when it emerged. He always took a Chinese and a Malay business tycoon who pretended to act as only interpreters, but were all hired by Whitehall to make their contribution to the peace effort in an endeavour to keep hold of the many businesses which were so lucrative and important. It worked well as word soon got around that the British Government intended to continue giving financial assistance to local companies when new local managers took over, providing the current markets were maintained. Without even knowing it, Barry and his team were part of the larger effort which was being made all over the country on a national scale to fend off the kind of offensive break from British rule which had been so damaging to other new countries which had been attaining their independence, especially in Africa

The time soon came for Barry's last days of shopping for souvenirs to take home. He enjoyed visiting the many Indian Emporiums in Singapore as he knew that he would find none of those little ivory statuettes in England. He soon stocked up with a few of the best ones and also a few cheap fans, lanterns, coasters, silk dressing gowns and local paintings. They all went into his tin trunk which was going be sent on by the army by sea to reach him in London shortly after his arrival without him having to pay much customs duty on the many things he had bought during his three years abroad. He wondered what they would think about the many tins of cigarettes which lined the bottom of the trunk which he had never found a home for. He would just have to smoke them all himself.

The officers in Barry's unit organised a fairwell party for him and all the civilian clerks and administrators were there. They put him through all the embarrassment of making him wear a huge floral wreath around his neck and soon they were all in good spirits and drinking the health of everyone there. Barry had always enjoyed working with them all as a good team, and they had always respected and helped him as they helped all the young officers who passed through the unit and then went home again as though it had all been a dream. They had taught Barry all about the local customs and traditions while he was there with them, and as a goodbye present they had bought him a "slow-boat-to-China" cooking bowl. They knew he had loved those long meals with hot coals in the small chimney in the middle of the dish to keep the liquid around it constantly boiling while meat, eggs and vegetables were added to it in the same manner as the Swiss fondu, but without any restrictions of what went into the dish. It had always been a pleasant way of spending an evening with much alcohol being passed around the table.

The journey home had been organised for him to be on one of the current troop-carrier planes. These were Hermes propeller aircraft equipped with all the seats facing backwards having their backs to the pilot. Barry was appointed as orderly officer for the troops on board. This was quite a serious responsibility as there were two overnight stops on the way home and Barry had to make sure that the other ranks found their way to the accommodation which had been reserved for them in Bangkok and Karachi when they put down there.

He enjoyed the overnight stops, because they allowed him a first glimpse of new places he had not had time to visit before. The first was Bangkok which he found to be hot, dusty and dirty, but unfortunately he did not have time to explore its many charms or to see any of the magnificent temples. It was also reputed to be a great place for cheap shopping and lively night life, but he had no time for any of that either, as all his free time was taken up by a meeting which had been arranged for him at a central hotel.

Karachi was quite different and seemed to be set in its old ways, and Barry could see quite clearly from the state of the people in the streets that there was considerable poverty there. The troops from his plane were all taken to "Mrs Minawallas Hotel", a huge monstrosity on the outskirts of the city. Maybe there was a Mrs Minawalla, but Barry didn't see her—nor was there anybody else trying to manage that monolithic ugly building of some fifteen stories. It had just been left empty above the second floor level and the troops were told that they should make themselves at home in any of the hundreds of spare rooms. The rooms all had one bed, a chair and one table, and that was all. There was reasonably clean bed-linen on the beds and small hand-towels were provided. All the men had been given packed meals and a bottle of fruit juice. The only staff consisted of a strange-looking scruffy Pakistani wandering around with a jug of tea and plastic cups. He was filthy dirty but then so was everything else in that dusty atmosphere. It was all very basic and the men couldn't wait to be on their way back to the plane again in the morning.

There was a refuelling stop in Nice, but no one was permitted to leave the airport and soon they were on their way again for the last leg of the journey to Northolt Airport in West London. Everyone was excited as none of them had been home for a long time, and for Barry it was all of three years. It had felt like thirty and he was a new man. During that time his father had returned from Germany and had joined his brother in the travel business which was doing well. He had also taken over his flat with his German girl friend whom he had now married. Barry was going to stay with them in the same flat which he had lived in with his uncle and aunt before he left them to get onto that troopship all that time ago.

The plane landed at about 4.0am but there were enough taxis to go round and everyone somehow found their way to where they wanted to go. The airport building emptied like magic without anyone needing any assistance. Barry was thrilled to be back in England and he even enjoyed the rain which he hadn't seen since the last monsoon season in Singapore—and that was quite a different sort of rain which poured down like stair rods. This was lovely cool English drizzly rain which he had not experienced for three years and had often dreamed about during those hot sultry nights in the tropical climate of Malaya. He was home again and feeling very strange as he knew that he was quite a different person from the boy who had left Liverpool on that troopship in that early morning mist three years ago.

The first pleasure was to meet his family again who were all waiting for him, and then he would go out into the world and do whatever he wanted. He felt confident that the army training which had been instilled into him would be beneficial in so many ways. But now he had to do all those little things he had missed, and which he had promised himself while he was sweating out there in the heat of those tropical jungles—like riding on the top deck of a double decker bus going down Oxford Street in the rain, or smelling roses in the park. He liked being back.

After a few days of getting used to being back home, Barry made contact with the authorities he had been briefed to report to, and was duly directed to a branch of the Foreign Office in Whitehall where he eventually met the civil servant who worked for someone who worked for someone else who wanted to thank Barry and inform him that they were grateful to him for his input and efforts in Malaya and that they would probably not be seeing him again. That was all. It was over.

THE END

Geoffrey

CHAPTER ONE

I don't know if I can do this but I will try, and you see if you can get it. The story really begins in Singapore where I was a young subaltern in the British Army attached to one of the many branches of General Headquarters situated on different parts of the island. We were engaged in backing up the requirements of our armed forces who were fighting the last of the communist terrorists "upcountry" in the Malayan jungles. Everyone knew that "the Emergency" (as it was called) was coming to an end and that independence would soon be given both to Malaya (which would then be called Malaysia) and to Singapore separately.

We were a fairly happy bunch in the mess considering that we were so far from home. There were seven of us bachelors living in which comprised junior officers from various regiments and supporting military units and we all had different supervisory jobs to do. These were ordained by senior officers higher up in the command, and the whole military operation was working smoothly as it had done for the past eight or nine years.

Most of us were pleased to be there as it was all a huge adventure for us in a totally different climate and general environment. Most of us were experiencing the tropics for the first time and living among people who were totally different from us in every possible way. On Singapore Island there were Chinese, Malays, Indians, Chi-chis (a mixture of colours) and a few Europeans working in the banks and large companies. Then there was the extreme heat. I was slowly getting used to the hot climate and following a completely new routine of life. This started quite early in the morning and then we all returned to the mess for lunch and took a long siesta in the afternoon. Fortunately all the officers' bedrooms had a large fan in the middle of the ceiling as the atmosphere was hot and damp and would otherwise have been unbearable. We each had our own houseboy who looked after us and cleaned our room and attended to our washing, which was so important as we changed our clothes at least twice a day.

There was a friendly atmosphere in the mess among the officers living there. Paddy was a large humorous captain in the Royal Artillery and he kept us amused most of the time when he wasn't looking after his troops or training for one sport or another. Then Taffy, who was my immediate superior officer was a captain in the Royal Engineers (or REME to be more exact) and always seemed to find work for all of us to do—well at least for half of every working day before it became too hot to do anything and we just faded away after lunch into our rooms.

Captain Osborne had just been sent home to the UK because his wife was divorcing him—and that was not acceptable in the officers' ranks in the army—and we were waiting for his replacement to arrive from Korea where our troops had been supporting the Americans in their war against the communist factions there. A truce had recently been declared on the basis that a line was being drawn between North Korea and South Korea which neither of them could cross—and then our troops could go home. Geoffrey was not so lucky as to be sent straight home though, as he still had to serve two years of his Far East posting. So in its wisdom the War Office decided to send him to join us in Singapore to help close up the activities there.

I remember that when he arrived I was just drying off after my shower after a good long siesta. I heard the grating noise of the three ton military truck drawing up outside the front of our mess. Geoffrey jumped out of the front seat where he had been sitting next to the driver and went round to the back of the vehicle to supervise his trunk being off-loaded and carried into the building.

Our "Number one" boy was quickly on the scene and quietly ordered two younger boys where to take the trunk, as he already knew which room had been allocated to the new officer arriving. Then he greeted Geoffrey with a bow and after exchanging a few pleasantries, showed him where his room was situated.

Geoffrey had the advantage of having been out East for a year, so he was already properly dressed in his tropical officers' uniform and did not need to be acclimatized as we had all been on our first days there. He was quite plump with a happy rounded face and straight blonde hair which kept flopping over his eye on one side until he flicked it back over his forehead. His clothes were wet with perspiration after his long journey, so he was looking forward to going to his new room to change them.

When Geoffrey had showered and changed into fresh clothes he joined us in the lounge. He was quickly introduced to all the officers present, and soon we were busily exchanging information about the various military activities going on in the area. Paddy was quick with his amusing cracks about how useless most of those activities were, and how we would all be more use directing the traffic down Oxford Street. That was Paddy and he was soon stamped on by Taffy who took his job as the senior officer present very seriously as the Welsh usually do. Anyway he knew that Geoffrey had been posted to his unit in the battalion and would therefore be taking orders from him, so he needed to get matters in the right perspective before the newcomer could be led to believe that he had joined a disfunctional unit. Taffy would never allow that to happen and started the way he meant to carry on—by being taken seriously—which of course always had the opposite effect and created considerable amusement in the mess.

The next morning after breakfast we all piled into the Land Rover which always collected us to take us to our various parts of the unit, and Geoffrey then got out with Taffy to go into his office for his first briefing and job description. The various offices were all temporary wooden buildings which were quite adequate in that heat, and we all had our own desks and supporting staff nearby. Young boys would soon appear with cups of coffee or whatever their uniformed bosses liked to drink, but this never got out of hand and Taffy made sure that all his supporting officers took their responsibilities seriously. He had a job to do and he would make sure that all his junior officers carried out their duties efficiently. This was the army and he never let us forget it. He was personally responsible to the colonel of the battalion for the duties allocated to him, and he fully intended to be considered favourably for promotion when his time came, without anyone under him letting him down.

I was lucky as a junior officer to be given a mobile job which enabled me to drive around the huge area occupied by our battalion checking on the various matters which the commanding officer had given orders to be done. I had my own Land Rover, and in that heat it was a pleasure to drive it around without any top on the vehicle. I visited most parts of the unit every day and so came into contact with all my fellow officers during my brief visits to check on the flow of various activities.

Geoffrey had been put in charge of the main clothes store which comprised a huge warehouse which was manned by a gang of mainly Chinese and Indian labourers. They spent nearly all their time carrying large boxes from one place to another when told to do so, or loading them onto the lorries which came to collect them for distribution up-country, so they were all scantily dressed and most of the men worked topless. The hot sun didn't seem to burn their tanned skins and none of them ever wore a hat. As the officer in charge of them Geoffrey was expected to wear his light uniform short-sleeved shirt, shorts and peaked officers' hat at all times—and always to carry his swagger stick as all of us officers did.

I got used to visiting Geoffrey on my rounds and he was always pleased to see me and to stop whatever work he was doing to have a brief chat. He was a "regular" officer and had joined the army by going to Sandhurst to train for his commission, so it was a career for him and not just two years' national service as with most of us—or perhaps a few short service types like me who had merely signed on for that extra year to obtain a few financial benefits. He was a captain now and was looking forward to being promoted and staying in the army for at least twenty years and then being pensioned off. That was his ambition.

Everybody soon liked Geoffrey as he was jovial and very communicative but never noisy or drunk. He was usually the first one in a group to offer a drink when we met in the mess before a meal, and you always felt that if you had a personal problem he was probably the first in the bunch that you would ask for advice. He was in his early thirties, which made him a little older than most of us junior subalterns, but then there were many captains and majors older than him in the unit. They all liked him, but didn't show it. That was not a place for favoritism and all the chores and duties were dished out by the colonel personally in a fair way. For example, I was always amused by his method of choosing the time when the Orderly Officer of the day had to turn out and inspect the guard on the main gate. He had his favourite pair of dice which he shook openly down the dining table at the end of every lunch. The period of duty began at 6.0pm, so if the numbers on the dice added up to seven or more, the duty officer was a lucky man and turned out the guard later that evening at the time shown on the dice, but if it was a smaller number then he would be turning them out early in the morning which was never popular.

Geoffrey was equally popular with his civilian workforce, and when I visited them in their warehouse on my rounds I always found them to be cheerful and hard at work with Geoffrey helping them as much as he could, not only by making the duties clear and sensible, but also by helping to lift some of the larger boxes which were too much for the smaller build of some of the Chinese and Malay boys. Taffy didn't like that and had told him to stop it, he told me, so he was a bit put out as he felt he was letting the boys down by just ordering them to lift things which he felt much more capable of handling. So he ignored the order and carried on helping out. He didn't take Taffy too seriously and couldn't believe that he really meant to be difficult. He was wrong. They were just two completely different characters, for while Geoffrey believed that as an officer he was duty bound to use his initiative and to give orders which he believed to be correct and proper in the circumstances, Taffy believed that junior officers should always obey the reasonable orders of their superior officers. He firmly believed that his order to Geoffrey was not only reasonable but essential to establish the superiority of all commissioned officers. Geoffrey was just letting the side down and could not be allowed to get away with his disobedience of a direct order. The next time Taffy caught Geoffrey helping his boys, he was hard at it and had gone further by taking off his shirt and hat to do the job properly. Taffy was furious and hauled him up for a serious reprimand and told him that it would go on his record as insubordination and disobedience of an order given by a superior officer. What none of us knew was that Geoffrey already had a black mark on his service record showing that he had been reprimanded for a similar offence in Korea before he joined us. There he had been helping some Korean workers lift a heavy object when his colonel had seen him do it and reprimanded him. He was very upset by the charge as he totally disagreed with it, but his superior officers were thinking differently and that was all there was to it. Now he only had to be reprimanded once more for a similar offence to make a total of three marks against his record for which he could be cashiered and made to leave the army with a black mark—and without any pension.

It didn't take long for Taffy to find Geoffrey in a similar position helping some workers with a job he had given them, but what made it worse was that he was clearly showing that he had no regard or respect for the order which had been given to him previously, as he had again taken off his shirt and was working side by side with the young Malay coolies under his command. He felt adamant that as he was the officer in charge of the packing unit he should be allowed to get on with it to the best of his ability. Taffy did not agree and hauled him up for the third reprimand and mark on his record sheet. That would be the end of his army career and Geoffrey knew it. He was angry, but when we all discussed it openly in the mess, it was generally agreed that perhaps the army was not the place for Geoffrey and he would do better to move on into civilian life where he could make his own rules.

Geoffrey on the other hand argued that if the elite senior officers in the British Army thought in that way, and seriously believed that commissioned officers should not stoop to help those under their command, then he would probably find that the English bosses of companies he applied to work for in civilian life would think the same way, and he would feel just as angry. He saw it as a serious matter of principle and he wanted nothing to do with it. He would not live in England he said, so he would go home to be demobilised and then go to live in Paris with his brother who was working there for NATO. He had no idea what he would be able to do for a living when he was out of the army and it seemed that he just didn't care. He believed that the Conservative government ruling England was making everyone change into money-grabbing businessmen which he didn't like, so that was another reason for not staying there.

Geoffrey wanted to live among people who cared for each other more, and not just be selfish trying to make a quick buck. He knew that the French government was also a right wing party, but he strongly believed that the French were basically more "left-wing" than the British, and that very soon there would be a change of government and the new prime minister would see that France once again became a socialist republic and a happier country to live in. He truly believed from his few visits to France that the people there had always been more social since the Revolution and that there was a spirit of togetherness which he believed in and hoped to find there.

CHAPTER TWO

I didn't hear about Geoffrey for about two years after that as I had to finish my own tour of duty in Singapore and complete the three year engagement in the army I had signed up for, but eventually I returned home to London and settled down finding work for myself in one or two different things. London had certainly changed during my absence, but it seemed to be much more lively than I remembered, but of course I had grown up without realising it. I had also gained my independence and was now sharing a flat with two other young men who were working in the City.

The time soon came for me to think about taking a holiday abroad, and as I had no close friends in London yet who wanted to go away anywhere with me, I arranged to visit Paris on my own and look up old Geoffrey and see how he was getting on. I contacted him to tell him I was coming over, and then made the train and hotel booking through my family's travel company who forgot to tell me that single rooms in Paris hotels were not usual, but anyway they had kindly arranged with a hotel they knew over there to look after me for those few days. When I arrived, the hotelier showed me into a converted bathroom—so that the bath could be made up as a single bed which was so unusual, but it made me laugh—and after my first alcoholic night out with Geoffrey and friends it really did not bother me. I had experienced worse in the jungle. It bothered Geoffrey though, and he was appalled and insisted that I should go and stay with him in his flat in Pigalle.

The flat was in one of those huge Parisian blocks which one enters through a front door which is opened with a magic number and then into a courtyard and then on into one of several other buildings each comprised of many flats. All of them overlooked the central courtyard on one side and roofs of Pigalle on the other side, and as that street was on a steep hill, one side of the flat was on the second floor and the other side of the flat was level with the sixth floor. Everything was very old and had that Parisian musty smell about it which was enhanced by the smell of Geoffrey's tobacco as he smoked strong french Gouloise cigarettes all the time with a short cigarette holder. He shared the flat with his younger brother, but we didn't see much of him as Johnnie worked long hours and was engaged to a local girl and spent most of his time in her flat.

Geoffrey hadn't changed a bit, and I could have sworn that he was still wearing the same shirt I had last seen him wearing in Singapore. Now he also wore a cravat but everything he did wear had that look of a style from the last century—clean but worn and out of date. He set about making tea in the old English way with a large teapot and biscuits on an old tray, and while he was doing this with such a sense of purpose and accurate detail with everything in its right place, I had the time to look around the sitting room and see his old momentoes, some of which had found their way from his room in Singapore. The waterworks in the flat were a disaster, but I was soon taught how to flush the toilet by standing on the seat and pulling the lever adjacent to the raised water butt. There was no bathroom as such, but there was a quaint old bathtub in the corner of the kitchen which was half the length of the ones we had at home and somewhat deeper. Any washing he had to do was hung on a line over the tub, so on some days you had to get out of the bath slowly and carefully not to take a faceful of wet towels and sheets with you. Taking a bath was a friendly matter anyway as Geoffrey would suddenly appear to boil the kettle at the other end of the room for the next inevitable cup of tea.

Geoffrey kept three cats and on my first visit I remember how one of these jumped onto my lap from nowhere and settling down there started to purr loudly. He was very friendly and obviously used to greeting people who visited the flat. Fortunately I rather like animals so I was not put out, which was just as well as Geoffrey soon appeared with the tea and started to talk to the cat as though it was a close friend who was understanding every word—in French of course. This was a French cat.

I soon learned that Geoffrey was now self-employed as a translator. His knowledge of French had become almost perfect, but he still preferred to translate from French into English and there was quite a high demand for that work—especially in the field of specialist magazines. His daily routine was to take the metro every morning across the city to some office on the Left Bank and spend a couple of hours working there before walking around the corner to a local brasserie for a light lunch with a demi of light French beer. So I joined him there later in the day. He told me that he had a few friends, but nobody special so he spent most of his time on his own, and after his lunch he always went home to feed the cat. That was his routine. It was clear to me that Geoffrey did not have a girlfriend and did not want one. In fact the only girl he ever spoke to me about with any kind of affection was one he had met in Korea all those years before, and then by the way he spoke about her made me wonder if she had come to a tragic end. He never spoke of her again. Of course there was always the possibility that Geoffrey could have homosexual tendencies, as he was so pleasant with everyone regardless of sex, but I soon put that out of my mind when I saw that he did not show any special tendency towards the same sex in the bars we visited. He liked everyone equally.

We visited many bars during my visits to Paris when I stayed with Geoffrey. Some of them became firm favourites of mine—especially those at the top of the hill around the Place du Tertre, even with all the tourists who engulfed them. I just loved to mingle with the artists there, many of whom had become friends of Geoffrey's. He knew everyone and everyone knew him but he was always alone. I always stayed with Geoffrey when I visited Paris—which must have been at least twice a year. I think he would have been offended if I had stayed anywhere else.

As the years went by it was obvious that he was doing nothing to improve the flat in any way. Perhaps he couldn't afford to redecorate it or to replace anything, but I never heard him even indicate that he wanted to. The same piles of books stayed put in exactly the same place on the shelves for all those thirty odd years I was visiting him. He continued to use the same chipped cups and even the same old beer mats to put them on. I liked that in a strange kind of way as it gave me a feeling of permanence somewhere in the world when everything was changing so quickly everywhere else. He continued to smoke like a chimney and to cough for half the morning, but I never saw him ill. He just took lots of tablets for all sorts of reasons, but I never saw any evidence of the necessity for this behaviour. He also continued to be optimistic about the fairness of the French Republic compared with the nasty British government, but as the years went by he voiced his disappointment with the present government and always insisted that the next election would put in the right people. Of course they never did and Paris never really changed.

Geoffrey never got a permanent job of any sort, but then he never seemed to run out of translating jobs which kept him in groceries and tobacco. He always refused to accept private offers of financial assistance as he felt very strongly that the government should make payments to anyone who earned less than a modest income, and he had clearly reached the age when he was receiving his pension from the State. So he continued to exist in this way and never complained. "Che sera sera" was his favourite motto. "What will be will be."

One day his brother Johnnie telephoned me from his new house in Portugal to tell me that Geoffrey had died quite suddenly. He was fifty. No accident, no illness—he just faded away. There would be no funeral he said because Geoffrey had made a Will stating categorically that there should not be one and that his body should be given to the local hospital for medical research. He was penniless and left nothing of any value.

So what was the point of this story? Well I am sure you have worked out that there wasn't one really—except to tell of the pleasure of knowing a truly decent and honourable man who always lived up to his own high standards—whatever the cost.

THE END

A Lawyer's Tale

CHAPTER ONE

There was the usual crowd of young oarsmen gathering in the bar of the rowing club after an outing on the river. They were looking clean and refreshed after a good hot shower and all feelings of exhaustion had long gone. The usual talk started about changes being made to various crews and expectations for regattas being planned for the rowing season about to begin.

The River Thames looked so peaceful and quiet as it flowed past the clubhouse. It was now devoid of all the sleek racing boats which had been brought ashore and were safely stacked in the boathouse. They were quickly replaced by a gathering of swans who were now in charge of the river again and not fearing for their lives with racing eights and fours which only a short time before had been challenging their right to rule the water. They looked so elegant with their long necks and clean white bodies gliding along together silently in formation. It was quite mesmerizing to watch them from the club balcony where several young men were taking their drinks to enjoy the peaceful setting.

Julian was chatting quietly with James who was another member of his rowing crew. James was a law student reading for the bar and knew that he had to go home soon to continue with his studies which he took very seriously, but he always liked to have a little break after his outing on the river before setting out on his journey home. Julian was very different as he had plenty of time on his hands and nothing to rush home for. He didn't have a career pathway at all having only recently come out of the army where he had been a young officer serving with the Gurkhas in Malaysia. He had only been back in London for a few months and was now helping with the family garage business. It was doing well and he felt he was helping to improve the business and making it even more efficient, but it didn't take much of his time and it certainly wasn't taking him anywhere. He didn't have any dreams or ambition to increase the business, so without realising it, he was really in a rut.

"What is it you actually do?" James was asking him just out of friendly interest, as he knew that his friend worked from home. "I mean where will your business take you? You seem to be a very intelligent sort of chap who could do well as a lawyer or an accountant or something!"

Julian grimaced as the more he spoke to his friends at the club the more he realised that he should really take up a career now that he had left the army. He didn't like the feeling of being left behind by friends who were really no more clever than he was. His parents had never spoken to him about it as he did not seem to care what he did, and his mother was a true Italian and no matter how much she loved him, she really knew nothing about the British system or how to advise her son about such matters. She was just happy to have him around helping with the business.

"You need to study for a career to get on in life!" James was saying. He was adamant that the world was run by people who had qualifications, and Julian had to admit to himself that although there were many examples of colourful individuals who had reached high places and made their millions without any degrees at all, in the main it was a good start which every man needed—and that meant qualifications if anyone was really ambitious or meant to get anywhere.

Julian had never even thought of studying for anything more after he had left school with his A levels. The army had considered those to be sufficient for a commission and he felt that he had done well serving as an officer for five years mostly in the Far East. James had a point though, and he knew that he should definitely think about it. After all he had plenty of time on his hands and was feeling that he needed some kind of goal which was sadly lacking in his life.

"Yes I'm sure you are quite right," he agreed somberly, ready to try anything. "Do you think you could help me?" James was a nice guy and he liked Julian and was determined to help him get onto some kind of pathway.

Julian thought that the law sounded like a good career—especially when he heard that he could study for the necessary exams by post. He was after all committed to helping his family and could not therefore think about leaving home to go to some university course. James gladly gave him all the information he needed and Julian was soon buying law books and joining a correspondence course which made him send answers to questions being sent to him at home.

After a few weeks Julian was finding out more about the career he had chosen, and the awful truth dawned on him quite slowly that he was actually embarking upon a five year study course which would lead him to the necessary bar examinations which he understood he could easily fail, as so many did. He wasn't daft, but even if he passed them, would he even then be suited for the profession? There were no other lawyers in his family, and he smiled to himself when it dawned upon him that he had probably been attracted to qualifying and being called to the bar simply because no one else in his family had reached such di zzy heights before. There were no professionals in his family even though some of them had done quite well in their various businesses. But he was thinking that if he passed all the exams and qualified as a barrister he would be part of the English Establishment—and perhaps he would then be looked up to by his father. Was that his intention? He never really went in for that kind of self-analysis but it did occur to him later.

The great disadvantage was that there was no one in the family who was prepared to back him up, and after a while it seemed that his father almost resented the fact that his son may do better in life than he had done. He never mentioned it, but the fact remained that he gave his son no support whatsoever and actually stopped communicating with him. Julian found this a bit odd, but hardly noticed it at the time as he was so busy studying. He never said anything anyway, so nobody knew or care and he just stopped speaking to his son. He had always been tight with his money and never made any offers to help Julian with his tutorial fees. Also when he wondered about the long silence, he felt that it was for his father to contact him, and not for him to chase after his father. Julian's mother was feeling that she had made a very good deal with her son, which was that he would continue managing the garage business while he was studying, and in return she only had to provide him with a basic salary for that period. They both agreed that it was for a fixed term of five years by which time he should have qualified and be self-supporting.

Julian stopped to think that perhaps he may not be suited for an academic career, so he decided to go to a Career Analysis Company which specialised in advising young people what they should do with their lives. He duly made an appointment and when he went to their office in the West End he was most impressed by their thorough system. He was given a sheet of paper with a long list of questions regarding his likes and dislikes of types of work and hobbies, to which he had to answer "Yes", "No" or "Maybe" by spiking a hole in the appropriate column as quickly as he could. There was no time for any long consideration of the simple questions, as each question had to be answered with an honest impulse, and he may in fact contradict a previous reply and therefore give away any uncertainties. These replies were fed into a computer which then produced several graphs showing aptitude, strength and knowledge to some extent, and the final graphs were studied by an expert who immediately showed them to Julian and explained to him what they meant.

"What it all comes down to" he said carefully, "is that you would probably do well as either a lawyer, music teacher or possibly an accountant. What do you think about that?"

Julian was overjoyed, as he had decided not to tell them about his legal study course, but now he could, after being so well backed up by their system.

"A barrister's course you say?" replied the elderly executive. "Oh no, that would not be a good idea! You see there are other parts of your character which are evident from these graphs, which show that you are not very confident about your opinions. Perhaps you didn't realise it, but you have often give different answers to similar questions. There is nothing wrong with that, and we all do it from time to time, but it seems that you are too open and often change your mind about things. Intelligent and thorough I can see you are, but not so sure of yourself as you need to be for the Bar. Those guys think quickly on their feet and they don't get a second chance when interrogating witnesses. Just imagine if you are in Court and you needed time to consider some point being made by the other side—and then changed your mind! No, that would not be good, and if you have begun studying for the Bar already, then you should take my advice and change tack to become a solicitor. I am sure you would be a good one!"

Julian took his advice and agreed to change his course of study. He stopped his barrister's course and then arranged to advertise in the Law Society for a firm who would take him on as a solicitor's articled clerk, and was soon visiting firms of solicitors who were offering positions to articled clerks to work with them while they studied. After only a few weeks he was being interviewed by a small firm in Lincoln's Inn who probably thought that as an ex-army officer he would introduce influential new clients to them. The pay was minimal, but the partners of the firm quickly told him that he was lucky not to be paying a premium which their parents had done years before and that the old system had only recently stopped being the way into the profession. The advantage to the underpaid articled clerks was that no one expected any real work from them, and they therefore spent most of their time idly lodging papers in the courts or drinking in the local pubs with other articled clerks. Julian was no exception and, as he had been in the last age group to be called up for National Service, he soon found that he was a few years older than most of the other articled clerks who had gone into the profession straight from school or university. This seemed to give him some seniority and authority over them which he enjoyed.

The mental pressure put on law students was hard as no failures were allowed in any of the subjects, and Julian was made to study harder than he had ever done before. He could have given up at any time, as so many of the students did, but he was determined to pass even if he had to take some of the subjects more than once. The best advice he received was from an old lawyer who had become a private teacher, and realising that so many students failed simply because they did not concentrate sufficiently and let their busy social lives get in the way, he organised "last mInute" legal courses in the Lake District. Julian joined his course and was pleased that he did not spoil the man's record of a one hundred per cent success rate. Looking back on his legal studies he recalled that the subjects which he had passed in were Constitutional Law, Contract Law, Trusts, Criminal Law, Land Law, Commercial Law, Probate Law, Divorce and Family Law, Equity, Accounts, Torts and Conveyancing.

Five years had gone by and after all that work, sweat and tears, Julian was on his own now, and very soon he began to realise that without any connections to help him, it was going to be difficult for him to find any clients or even a good job. None of his family had the remotest idea of how the profession was run. So once again it was a chance remark made by one of his rowing chums at the club which made him apply for a job as assistant solicitor to a large international insurance company who took him on immediately. He was very happy with that as he had never really thought about going into private practice.

He attended the formal ceremony to receive his Admission and first Practicing Certificate from the Master of the Rolls in the Law Society's Hall in Chancery Lane. None of his family came with him or even sent any messages of congratulations. It was quite a grand event with the Master of the Rolls appearing in his full regalia and Julian was thrilled and very impressed as he stepped forward to receive his certificate and be shaken by the hand of the great judge.

"Are you already with some big firm in the city?" the judge asked in a kindly way.

"No sir," Julian replied. "I am with an international insurance company in the West End."

"Well keep them on the straight and narrow!" said the judge with a smile handing over the scroll of parchment.

Julian remembered the kind words of the judge later when the insurance company found itself in such trouble a year of two later and had to go into liquidation. The International Life Insurance Company was part of a large group of companies, and Julian had started working in their head office in London. This entailed corresponding with other offices all over the world and he found the work fascinating. He met many interesting people in the legal department and often went out after work with Edward who was one of his colleagues and was becoming a real friend. Edward was slightly younger and married but more settled in his ways than Julian.

As time went by it became clear that the Company was not only unpopular with the other big city insurance companies, but also that its first share issue in the Stock Market was doomed to failure and the Company would have to fold. All the employees would simply become unemployed. Julian and Edward discussed the seriousness of the position with the other lawyers and all agreed that they should leave the Company before it went into liquidation and stopped paying them.

They all went out to dinner together and laughed about the situation as they all felt that as lawyers they should each be able to find other jobs quite easily. Julian was not so sure, and anyway he had a hankering to travel to Italy to see his mother's family and catch up with a favourite girl friend Annabella who had gone back to Rome with her parents. Nevertheless they all enjoyed the party and went on through the night with Julian finishing up in a very bad state in some underground club in Soho. He didn't remember how he got home.

CHAPTER TWO

Julian awoke the next morning with a severe hangover and after he got over that and was in a more somber mood he suddenly realized that he had never in his life experienced real freedom before, having been sent from one boarding school to another and then straight into the army to do his national service. Now he had lost his first job, he had no family, and did not even have a girl friend in England.

He made a quick decision to go away somewhere—just to get out of England. "Away?" he thought. "Where is away?" He looked through the newspapers for inspiration, and suddenly it occurred to him. The Munich Beer Festival! He was not a big beer drinker, but he needed a party, and he remembered meeting some German law students from Munich only a year or two before who had told him all about it and Wolfgang, who was the most friendly one of them, had left his address and personal details with him. So much to Wolfgang's surprise he received a telephone call from Julian announcing that he was going to descend upon him in Munich within the next few days. He would stay there for a few days to enjoy the festival and then think about going on to Italy.

Julian was now almost penniless, but he knew an estate agent who specialized in letting flats and when Julian telephoned him, he immediately promised to rent out Julian's flat and pay the money into his bank so Julian could feel reasonably secure that there was something there to fall back on, and he was happy to advance Julian enough cash to tide him over his travel expenses.

The cost of the coach trip to the beer festival was minimal and included staying in a camp site nearby. Julian had been an enthusiastic boy scout a few years before, but he found the atmosphere at this camp site quite different and most distasteful as most of the campers seemed to be penniless tramps of all ages who apparently could not afford the price of a hotel and therefore needed to stay there. They did not seem to be enjoying the camping experience at all as he had done in his boy scout days, and they were definitely not hygienic or even good company, so Julian decided to move into Wolfgang's flat and promised to occupy his sitting room settee for only a few days while he decided upon a plan.

He telephoned his girl friend Annabella in Rome and was thrilled to receive such a warm response from her. She had apparently been waiting for his call and was overjoyed to hear that he was on the way to see her. Suddenly the world was a lovely place, and he had something to look forward to. Somebody wanted him, and he was experiencing feelings he could not remember before. Very much in a positive frame of mind, he wandered around the Mercedes garage in Munich looking at the second hand cars which were for sale. He had no idea what he could buy, as that would all depend on how much money he could borrow. He made a quick calculation of how much a young man should earn in a mediocre job and then decided how much of that he could save to pay for a motor car. He worked out that if he borrowed about five thousand pounds from his bank he should be able to repay it within about six months if he found a job somewhere—even if it was only washing dishes. But would his bank manager agree?

He had soon decided which car he wanted within this price bracket, and fortunately the sales manager was not only friendly, but also spoke good English and did not mind making a telephone call to Julian's bank in London to help with Julian's request to ask for a loan. It all went like clockwork and feeling very positive, Julian asked for the latest radio and cassette player to be fitted to the car before he was driving his lovely second-hand Mercedes out of the garage with all the necessary paperwork having been completed. He was on his way to Rome and a new life.

The journey through Italy was magical, as not only did Julian enjoy the beautiful landscape and warm climate, but he also had a new feeling of being wanted by a lovely girl and her family. They were waiting for him and he could not wait to see them. He drove through the Alps playing his favorite classical music on the car cassette player and enjoyed all the sights as his route took him through Milan, Bologna, Florence and many beautiful Italian villages on both sides of the autostrada leading him to Rome.

He was met with open arms and many kisses from his beloved Annabella and to his delight and astonishment he found that he had been booked into the nearest hotel—and all paid for by her family. Annabella was the typical Italian beauty with her long black hair and lovely big black eyes and she took every opportunity to be close to Julian and to hold his hand or have her arm around him. He reciprocated fully and felt very much wanted and loved. They were going to have a lovely time together and Julian could not bear to think of moving on anywhere else.

The next few weeks were like a wonderful dream to Julian, and the loving couple were never separated. One fact which made the whole experience so much easier for Julian than he could have expected, was that Annabella's father Giuseppe had so enjoyed his time in England working for the Italian government there, that he had become completely anglicized and insisted upon his family speaking English which they had all learned there. This would inevitably slow down Julian's speed in learning Italian, but there were more urgent matters to deal with now and he could catch up with his language later.

Julian needed to find a job, and he soon found out how difficult that was, as the legal profession in every country is very different and each country has its own laws. Lawyers are just not interchangeable no matter how friendly the countries may be. He called upon many of the top Italian lawyers in Rome and they all showed great kindness and patience in doing so, but they were mostly nonplussed at why a young English lawyer should want to work outside his own country.

Julian was determined to find work in the city as his feelings for Annabella had grown stronger and he did not want to leave Rome at all. He found his way to the British Council which was staffed entirely by British nationals. At first they just ignored his request and told him that so many English travellers fell in love with Rome and tried to find work there as Julian was doing, so they had a policy of never helping anyone to find a job in the city as they would then soon be inundated by such requests which was not part of their job. But then one of them listened to his serious plight and when she realised that he was serious about settling in Rome and marrying an Italian girl, she offered to help him with his romantic situation and asked him to come back the next morning.

He was there at opening time and they walked down the street together and across a huge playground into a school building where the headmistress was waiting for them. She asked Julian a few questions in English and seemed to be pleased with his replies. Julian did not realise it at the time, but she was actually impressed that he spoke English without any accent or dialect and should therefore be a great help with her senior English students and their pronunciation.

It all started very well and Julian got on well with the senior students who were serious about improving their English, but it did not take long before the teaching staff were abusing his assistance and asking him to take on classes with much younger pupils who spoke no English and did not hesitate to make Julian's life a misery with their bad behaviour and pranks carried out at his expense. Suddenly Julian was experiencing at first hand what school teachers had to put up with, and he had a huge new respect for the teachers he had given such trouble to at his old school.

Julian's love for Annabella had blossomed over the passing weeks and months and he had taken over a small modern flat in a modern block very near to her parents whom he visited every day. They all had dinner together at least three times a week when Julian enjoyed the strong family feeling of love and consideration for each other. It made him wonder where his family had gone wrong as he had never experienced such a pleasant home atmosphere. The loving couple enjoyed exploring the old city together and in addition to his teaching, Julian had started a new business of finding holiday apartments for British holidaymakers. It all seemed to come together so easily when they were driving along the coastline and saw how many lovely holiday houses were empty and just boarded up for the winter months—which for Italians seemed to mean the whole year except for August. They quickly looked into the prospect of renting a few houses in the off-season months and arranging to advertise them on the English market. It all came together so quickly with the assistance of villa agencies in London who were so pleased to find an English representative on Italian soil.

Some evenings the loving couple just strolled through the Borghesi Gardens and looked down over the Piazza del Popolo, or otherwise walked to the other side of the Gardens to stop for a coffee in one of the glass covered cafes on the Via Veneto. At least once a week they drove across the Tiber to the old district of Trastevere for a pizza in one of the small bars there, or to visit the English cinema hidden in the backstreets behind the Piazza Santa Maria. Another favorite walk was up the hill behind the huge memorial to the last King of Italy, Vittorio Emanuelle which the British Army during the war had so irreverently christened "The Wedding Cake". Perhaps because it looked like one . . . It was so peaceful up there overlooking the Forum of Rome with its delicate floodlighting throwing shadows between the old relics which could tell so many colorful stories of those ancient Roman days.

As a British subject it was necessary for Julian to post his bans of marriage on the wall of the British Consulate, and as the document included his occupation as "Lawyer," this came to the attention of the staff who were often pestered by British citizens with legal queries which they could not help with as they did not have any lawyers on the staff. The document gave

Julian's address in Rome, so it was not long before he was receiving visits from British subjects looking for legal advice on some problem back in England which was troubling them.

He was happy to give any advice, although he knew that he could not act as a practicing solicitor, as he was outside the boundaries of the UK. So he made sure that any case which actually did require the services of an English solicitor were directed to a firm he knew in London so that they were acting for the client and he was only paid for the work he did in Rome. He was an agent more than a solicitor but it seemed to be helpful to everyone that he knew all about the English legal system, and he was happy to be able to keep his hand in and not forget all the law he had learned so recently. It all worked well and Julian was paid good fees for advising clients and directing them when necessary to the doors of friendly solicitors in London—especially to arrange divorces which were not legally possible in Rome at the time.

Julian and Annabella had a fairytale wedding and enjoyed a honeymoon in Sicily. When they returned to Rome they moved into a new flat and started an Italian style married life. Julian left the school where he had been helping, as he had found an American investment company in Rome who needed assistance with their legal documents. His job also extended to showing interested American buyers around Italian properties for sale. This was much more fun for him, and fitted in very well with his other business of finding holiday homes for English families in the spring and summer months. It was all going very well and Annabella had also found a job with an Embassy which kept her busy, but they both knew that the time was coming when they should decide whether or not they wanted to settle down and live in Rome permanently. They both felt that Julian had worked so hard to qualify as a solicitor in England that it seemed a pity and a waste of all that work for them to go on living in Rome where he was not even able to fully make use of his qualification.

They struggled with the decision as they had a good life there. His success had grown and he was being recommended by many clients to others. Rome was the centre of the Italian film world then, especially with so many "Spaghetti Westerns" being churned out by the Italian studio at Cinecitta, so there were many famous actors visiting the city to make films. Dirk Bogard was one of those, and although he had his Italian advisors, he did not completely trust Italians, so he asked the British Consulate to recommend an English lawyer and eventually made an appointment to see Julian.

He was shown into Julian's office and after being formally introduced, he simply asked:-

"Are you a film lawyer, Julian?" and upon receiving a firmly negative response, he stroked his chin as only Bogard did with some aplomb, and said quite forcefully:-

"Well you are now!" and closed the subject by explaining very clearly and precisely what he wanted to have checked, together with full names and telephone numbers of leading Italian film lawyers who would be pleased to help Julian should he require advice or assistance. They were and he did. What was more, he found that odd calls were being made to him by supposedly genuine contacts with the Mafia which was the underground organisation which was supposed to be keeping some kind of law and order behind the scenes. The trouble was that no one knew who was a part of the organisation as it was strictly illegal. But this was Italy. They had the power and were apparently informed of Julian's new connections and this led to many strange incidents which Julian soon learned to keep quiet about. On one occasion when he was taking Annabella out to dinner, some stranger approached them at the entrance to the restaurant and insisted on introducing them to the MaitreD of the restaurant who immediately ushered them with a knowing wink to the best table with a specially ingratiating bow. "They" were getting to know him, and secretly Julian had to admit that he quite enjoyed the position of being recognised in a foreign country. It was only in small things, but they matter when you are a stranger in a foreign country, like being offered the best seats in a full restaurant, an extra bottle of wine or even a second cup of coffee and cognac for no charge—with a wink. The family looked after its own.

Away from that privileged world the Italian system continued to operate in its old style, so when Julian was asked to help a well known old Italian aristocrat to register his divorce with the government agency (the Anagraphe) as the Italian system required him to do, from one English lady and subsequent legal marriage to another English lady, the amorous Count was told by the police that if he did not complete the registration within two months, he would be arrested and charged with bigamy. This should have not presented any difficulty—save that when Julian made his application to the local Court for him, the clerk to the District Judge informed Julian that there were unfortunately no free dates available during the next two months for the judge to attend to the matter—unless of course a suitably large financial present was made . . . . It was and the new marriage was duly entered as legitimate. The Count was very grateful and showed his appreciation not only with a generous payment, but also in true Italian style by inviting Julian and Annabella to stay at his lovely villa in Porto Cervo, a beautiful resort on the north coast of Sardinia.

A few of Julian's old friends from London popped in to look him up in Rome as he had been easy to locate through the agent in London who had been letting out his flat. Edward made a habit of popping into Julian's office every time he visited Rome which had become quite frequent, and it was not long before he was asking Julian to introduce him to friends in Rome. He worked for a property investment business based in the Caribbean now and he knew that wealthy Italians were finding it difficult to invest their money in Italy and were keen to find a home for their savings abroad. Julian didn't trust him completely so he did not invest any money himself, but he saw no reason for not introducing him to Italian acquaintances and investors who may want to.

One of those was Andrea who was always popping into the office and seemed to be making deals with people who were totally unknown to Julian, but it seemed to make Andrea quite wealthy as he was always giving big parties in his house and at weekends on the beach. He had many American friends in Rome who also liked to show off their wealth so it was a perfect match.

Julian took Andrea to meet Edward in the bar of the Grand Hotel which seemed to have the right atmosphere for business meetings and they got on very well and promised to include Julian in any financial profit they made together.

"Two hundred houses will be built on one of the loveliest beaches in the Caribbean," Edward was saying. "Just look at these lovely photos of the place! Prospective buyers are already signing purchase contracts, but we still need more operating capital to complete the construction!"

"Well you can count me in!" Andrea said emphatically. "Just let Julian have a copy of your contract to look at and I will work out how much I can spare to invest. That interest rate is certainly more than I can get from any other investment here in Italy."

Within a few days the deal was made, the contract signed and a large amount of money paid over by Andrea to Edward. Julian had made a separate private contract with Andrea, but there was nothing further he could do but wait to hear from Edward about the progress of the development and when payments were made to the investors. He heard nothing further from Edward who he knew spent much of his time travelling so he did not expect to hear very much, but he became concerned when he heard from mutual friends that Andrea had disappeared. Nobody knew where he was or where he had gone to.

Months went by and eventually Julian and Annabella were making plans to return to London as Julian's agent there had told him that his flat was now vacant again. They had been getting tired of the chaotic Roman way of life and it was really only Annabella's parents living there who had caused them to stay so long, but they fully understood that Julian had to return to his own country sometime to take up the career he had worked so hard for, and anyway they would visit each other from time to time.

CHAPTER THREE

Back in London Julian soon found himself working for another large company, but this time it was in the construction business and he was again one of half a dozen lawyers employed to do the legal work. He enjoyed being back home. It always amused him to tell the story later of how he had stepped into one of his favourite old bars after being away for over three years only to find that it was exactly the same as it had been before—with the same old guys around the bar—and one of them had looked up and recognised him. He immediately announced to the other old regulars around the bar,

"Well if it isn't old Julian!"

Whereupon one of the others dryly replied, "Oh yes? Well it's his round isn't it?" and continued reading his newpaper.

Julian smiled and at once felt he was home again.

Lawyers working for his new company had a very exalted position as the directors knew well that they could have earned much more in private practice. It was therefore agreed that they could do private work in addition to working for the Company providing the Company was always put first in their priority. Private clients were therefore often admitted into the Company's building to visit their lawyer for a legal conference.

Julian built up quite a client base in this way and managed to keep up with some old friends in Rome, but he had never managed to track down Edward again and wondered what happened to him and to Andrea's money. He was still waiting for his commission to be paid so he would not be losing sight of his rights to claim on his contract with Edward and Andrea if he could ever find them.

Three months went by before he heard from old friends in Rome that Andrea's body had been found. He had evidently been murdered some weeks before somewhere on the beaches near Rome where he had a country house. The police were very dilatory in such cases where they suspected that the

Mafia may be involved—which was always the case when big money was concerned. No questions were asked and the whole thing was hushed up.

Julian was very concerned as he had no way of finding out who was responsible, or even whether there was any connection between the murder and the investment with Edward, who had also not appeared. He had a vested interest though, so he started trying to track him down through the agencies in the Caribbean where there should be some report on the progress of the development scheme which he had been selling.

Meanwhile he was having a good life in London with Annabella and they were thinking of branching out into the countryside. One of the many perks made available to senior staff of the Company (as with many others) was the offer of easy short term mortgages to enable staff members to buy homes. Julian and Annabella had their flat in Chelsea, but they were thinking of finding a second home in the country as they were both tired of the weekend routine of going to the local pub with friends at weekends when actually neither of them were big drinkers and neither of them enjoyed being drunk or even being with drunk friends. So they decided that they would find a place in the country within easy reach of London.

Julian drew a circle on the map a hundred miles around central London and then divided it into segments. He then listed the main estate agents in each segment and wrote to each one asking for lists and details of small country houses available for sale under the top price which he had agreed with Annabella they could afford to buy with a mortgage.

They enjoyed the next few weekends exploring one segment after another to look at the properties they had been offered. They started in Buckinghamshire simply because they had been invited to visit some old friends there, but finding nothing they liked, they moved on the following weekend to look at properties in the next segment. This went on weekend after weekend completing the circuit around the capital until they were back in Bucks again. It was all great fun with a purpose, but they had almost giving up finding anything they liked in the right price bracket.

Then one Sunday they were driving up a small side road in the countryside when they saw a "For Sale" sign at the bottom of the drive leading up to a poor-looking old farmhouse. Julian stopped the car and as they walked up the muddy drive to the house, he took in the view. It was magnificent, overlooking green fields and up to a gorgeous hill with absolutely no houses anywhere to spoil the beautiful rural landscape in any direction.

"This is it!" he whispered excitedly to Annabella who gave him a strange look. Was he mad? Her high-heeled shoes were already covered in mud.

"But the house is terrible!" she replied, and could not understand why he just smiled back at her. The door was being opened by a friendly old lady who told them that unfortunately the house was under offer so she could not help them. Julian was not to be put off.

"Have you exchanged contracts then?" he asked her pleasantly.

"Oh no!" replied the old lady. "Not yet, but my solicitors have the matter in hand and you should write to them if you are interested."

"Well that could take weeks!" replied Julian "And the buyer may not even proceed, so if you would like to sell your house quickly, my wife and I have decided we would like to buy it now, and as I am a solicitor I promise we would not mess you about. In fact I am going to give you a cheque for the deposit right now and you can pass it to your solicitor tomorrow. Will you agree to do that and then we can all save time?"

The lady was completely thrown off balance by the positive offer being made to her and she just stood there while Julian got out his cheque book and without any further conversation he wrote out a cheque for ten per cent of the asking price and wrote on the back of it his name and address and the words "Subject to contract".

"That should do it!" he said with a flourish as he handed it to her and quickly wrote down on the back of an envelope her name and details of her solicitor and the agent which he thrust into his pocket.

"Well I don't know!" she said smiling and disappearing inside the house.

Julian grabbed Annabella by the arm and steered her towards the car.

"What are you doing?" she gasped looking at him in bewilderment.

"Let me explain" Julian said quietly. "Location is everything, and we haven't seen anything as good as this all around London! I don't mean the house—I don't care about that as we can make whatever alterations we like, but the position is fantastic . . . . !"

Annabella was in a trance as she was now wondering if her husband had committed them both to something they may regret later. He put her at ease during their long drive back to London, and explained that they didn't have that kind of money in the bank anyway, and unless his boss at work agreed to the company backing them financially the whole deal would be off and the cheque cancelled, as he had marked it "subject to contract". She was beginning to understand now and gave him a big kiss on the cheek. She could leave it to him and it was all very exciting.

Julian's boss was true to form, and after he had heard all the details about the property, he wasted no time in having an agreement drawn up for Julian to sign while he wrote out a cheque to cover the amount Julian needed to exchange contracts. The deal was that the Company would pay for the house to make sure the purchase went through, and Julian would find an appropriate mortgagee to replace the Company loan within six months. In fact it took him less than six weeks. Big rich companies knew how to look after their staff and keep them happy.

As soon as contracts were exchanged the little old lady moved out of the house and down to Devon. This left the house clear for Julian to make immediate alterations. He had been making enquiries locally and had found a builder who was prepared to knock the ground floor of the house right through so that he could immediately start with the decorations. The whole thing only took about two weeks and suddenly there they were in their own country house—with a garden outside that was covered in rubbish and left-overs from the chicken farm which it had once been. That would take him a little longer, but he didn't mind. He needed a project and this one would be most enjoyable.

CHAPTER FOUR

Life changed dramatically for them as every weekend they rushed down to the country house which soon became known as "the Cottage". There was so much to do, and they were both new to it as neither of them had ever owned a house before, and neither of them had ever lived in the countryside before. Annabella loved to watch the rabbits playing at the bottom of the garden and Julian was happy to see how he was progressing in clearing the garden of all the rubbish and planning where to plant various flowers and vegetables.

It was only a small house, and Julian could well understand Annabella's misgivings about buying it, but she soon changed her mind when she realised how quickly they were changing the entire atmosphere of the place. When the new carpet went down she felt that the house was transformed into a palace—and she loved it.

They had met a few people in the nearest village and it was not long before Julian found the nearest pub. He was not a big drinker, and that was why he had really decided to leave the London scene, but nevertheless it was where everybody met and he was soon introduced to the chimney sweep and all the other trades he needed to assist with problems he encountered in doing up the house. What he had not realised was that there was a "quid pro quo" or tit-for-tat and he would be expected to help local people with their small legal problems.

He made it clear to his new friends that he came down to his new little house at weekends to escape from legal work, but nevertheless he did enjoy his work and he never failed to listen to peoples' problems and tried to help them if he could. The people here were quite different from the ones he worked with, so he had to admit to himself that he did enjoy helping with personal problems which were always quite different from the ones he dealt with at the office every day.

Ernie was well over eighty years old and he always appeared in the bar wearing the same old tattered clothes and looking as though he hadn't washed or shaved for a week, but he was a lovely guy and everyone enjoyed his good humour and local banter. Julian soon learned that he kept chickens behind a house nearby and that he was very knowledgeable about them and reared them in large quantities. He slid up to Julian at the bar one evening and pulled a tattered scrap of paper out of his dungarees.

"Oy Jules" he started quietly with his lovely local dialect in an embarrassed kind of way, "Ye be a lawyer ain't yer? Well just look at this which I got sent!"

He handed the scrappy sheet of paper to Julian who unfolded it and saw that it was a formal Notice which had been sent by the County Council to Mr Ernest Drummond at his home address demanding that he stop his cockerels from making a noise early in the morning failing which he would be prosecuted. He read it again and then turned to Ernie.

"Just how long have you had chickens in your house Ernie?" he asked.

"Oh about forty year now Jules" he replied.

"Ever had any complaints before?"

"No, never—well until they built that block of flats next to me two year ago. A few of them shout out of windows sometimes, but I take no notice."

"Mmmmm" Julian was thinking fast. "Look, you will have to reply to this Notice or the Local Authority will apply for a Court Order for you to dispose of your chickens."

"They can't do that surely? After all this time?" he was speechless with shock. "They be my life!"

"Don't you worry Ernie" Julian replied sympathetically. Leave the Notice with me and I will reply to the Council for you, but you will probably have to come to Court with me in a few days time. Is that OK?"

"Well yes OK as long as I don't 'ave to lose me chicks!"

Julian went to his office the next day and drafted a formal reply to the Notice to be sent to the Local Authority. He was just within the specified time, so now it was for the Local Authority to decide whether to withdraw the Notice or to proceed with it in the Magistrates Court. If they did, then Julian would be ready with witnesses to show that Ernie had been keeping chickens on his property long before the complainant had even bought his adjoining property.

Julian was feeling angry on behalf of Ernie, so a couple of days later he telephoned the Legal Department in the Local Authority office to ask whether they had received his reply to the Notice and what they would be doing about it. The clerk replied by saying that they had to proceed with all applications so they would be setting the case down for hearing shortly.

Julian was aghast as he felt that the law was so strongly in favour of Ernie's position that the Local Authority should have had the sense to drop the case rather than risk the legal costs which (if they lost the case) would have to be borne by the ratepayers, so he telephoned the BBC studio and asked to speak to Esther Ranson. She was a broadcaster who had become famous for running a series of amusing programmes poking fun at real problems in Society and usually belittling companies and various authorities for some obviously stupid decisions they had made. She always had some amusing footage showing the accused suspect running away from her interviewer or somehow making his guilt only too clear. The Law Society didn't like her at all, as she was obviously by-passing the legal system completely and sitting as judge and jury in every case she dealt with, but in the main she brought many injustices to the public eye.

The BBC operator took his telephone number and Julian thought he would hear no more, but that afternoon the lady herself called him back and listened to his story with considerable interest. It was apparent that she didn't like Local Authorities either. She politely asked for the full details of Julian's legal authority in saying that Ernie had the right to keep his noisy chickens, so Julian recited the famous case on the subject when Lord Denning had given a judgment which summed up the situation of a man who complained about a cricket team playing next to his house every week who—far too often—caused damage when they hit a cricket ball into his glasshouse. On appeal to him Lord Denning had made it quite clear in his judgment that as the man had "gone to the nuisance" and the nuisance had not gone to him, he would make no order for the cricket team to stop playing, but they did have to pay for any damage they caused.

Esther soon discovered that Lord Denning had retired, but with her zealous attention to detail she discovered his telephone number in the West Country and called him to check on the truth of the matter. The old judge was very happy to confirm Julian's summary of his case and passed on his regards to the lawyer who had remembered his case so well.

Now Esther was in her element and devised an amusing sketch for her next programme to be televised. She called Ernie and asked him to bring two noisy cockerels to her studio where she would film him arguing with two of her young assistants dressed in a very silly way to impersonate dull and stupid clerks from the Local Authority who were trying to argue that the cockerels should be kept quiet in the early morning. The noisy cockerels dominated the show, and Ernie was marvellous talking to them and arguing with the actors playing the part of silly-looking young civil servants and everyone in the studio took to him. The show was very amusing and a great success and probably damaged the reputation of the Local Authority considerably.

The case still went on in the Magistrates Court where apparently everyone including the Magistrate had seen the television skit and were determined not to by cast by the local papers as looking so stupid, so it was no surprise when the application by the Council was dismissed with all costs ordered to be paid by them. Julian submitted a bill which was promptly paid by the Local Authority and he was happy to make it clear to Ernie that he could keep his chickens without any further problems or interference from his neighbours.

Ernie always felt that he owed something to Julian even though it had been made quite clear to him that all costs had been paid by the Council. So every time Julian went down to the Cottage there was a package of two dozen fresh eggs on his doorstep.

CHAPTER FIVE

New cases were being brought to him every week and not all of them were Company matters. As head of the Legal Department, Barry made it clear that so long as Company work came first then any of his solicitors were perfectly free to use their time to help whoever they wanted. One defendant who had received a legal notice sent by Julian on behalf of a private client recognised the telephone number at the head of the covering letter as being that of the construction company, and fully believing that he could get Julian into trouble for "moonlighting" he telephoned the Company to make a complaint to the Managing Director. He put the call through to Barry who answered the man quite calmly to the effect that he was so pleased to note that the solicitor who had sent him the Notice was evidently spending most of his time in the Company's offices for him to be quoting that telephone number on his privately headed paper. The man had been put in his place and Barry was pleased to tell Julian that he would have no further trouble.

Julian was finding that more and more private cases were being brought to him by members of the staff, but so long as he had the time available he was pleased to be able to help. His reputation was growing.

One day his secretary Penny told him that her boyfriend Terry was in trouble with the landlords of his block of flats because he had given a late night party in his flat which had caused some damage for which they were seeking hefty compensation. Evidently the party had gone on late into the night, and when the neighbours complained, all the drunken guests decided to leave together at some very unfriendly hour in the morning. About ten of them squeezed into the lift together to take them down from the fifth floor of the building to the ground level. The lift had a maximum capacity of five persons for a good reason, because when it was overloaded it speeded up and so passed the ground floor level. That is exactly what happened in this case when the lift was so overloaded. The gates would then not open and panic spread among those drunk young people who were unable to move or get out of the lift, so someone pressed the Alarm button. This was connected to the local Fire Station who sent a Fire Engine immediately. Those firemen spared nothing as it was their job to save lives and they completely destroyed the lift gates to make sure that everyone got out safely.

The landlords sent a bill to Terry for the costs of repair to the lift, but he felt that the cost should be borne by the Insurance Policy covering the building and paid for by all the residents. They took the matter to the County Court where they met Julian who represented Terry and won the case for him, but each side had to pay their own legal costs as the Court decided that Terry was at least partially to blame for the accident.

Penny was thrilled that her boy friend did not have to face such an expense as the repair to the lift would have been, but he could not afford to pay Julian's heavy solicitor's fees either. She told Julian that Terry worked for a timber company, and almost jokingly suggested that he could pay Julian's fees with a delivery of timber. It so happened that Julian was at the time wondering how to construct a shed in the grounds of his new country cottage, so when he told Penny this, it did not take many days before Julian found a huge pile of lovely pine "tongue and groove" planks delivered to the front of his house.

This gave Julian some ideas about how to develop his property with very little expense, so he decided that his next project would be to construct a swimming pool. A member of the surveyors' department had been to see him for some advice regarding his pending divorce, and when Julian told him about his plan they were soon spending more and more time together over detailed plans for a private swimming pool to be put into the ground adjoining Julian's new little house in the country.

The next step would be to find a way to buy the actual materials, but then Julian discovered that his Company never used the same building materials twice, so in fact all he had to do was to arrange for some of the better quality used materials to be delivered to his house. Then he would just have to put them all together. It was all hard work but very practical and successful. He was surrounded by very pleasant advisors.

Every weekend he went down to his little country house and worked hard either decorating some part of the house, or if the weather was clear he was outside working in the hole in the ground which he was turning into the swimming pool. The ground was all rock chalk, so he had to hack away until he had the correct dimensions to put in the steel rods which would form part of the reinforced concrete when all was ready. Those were busy times for Julian as he was always in his office on time and always had piles of work to attend to.

Julian met Derek in the local pub occasionally on his way home, but he never seemed to know anything about where his old friend Edward had got to, but was not surprised that he had not bothered to settle his debt to Julian for introducing Andrea. He had a reputation for being a bit of a sharp character. The matter of Andrea's death was still a mystery, but Derek knew nothing about it. Then one day Edward just walked into Julian's office unannounced. He had tracked him down somehow and was clearly troubled.

"I heard about Andrea" he admitted with some concern. "Of course my contacts in Rome think that I had something to do with it, but that is rubbish!"

"Well it sounds a bit strange that he should be bumped off just after he has invested in your project!"

"Yes, I know," Edward admitted with a frown, "But it was nothing to do with me, and I am quite concerned that no one has made any claim for the return of Andrea's investment. What should I do?"

"I think you should go back to Rome and try to find out who is handling Andrea's estate as his money should be passed to someone. He wasn't married was he, so it could be quite difficult to track down his beneficiaries. Anyway that would be the correct thing to do."

"I am just thinking that if no one has made any enquiries perhaps they don't care about his investments and are just writing them off!"

"Then you would be stealing his money!" Julian exclaimed.

"Well I may just as well keep it as go to a lot of trouble trying to find some distant relation in Italy who doesn't even know about the investment. I am sure that is what any Italian would do!"

"So if that is what you think why have you come to see me about it?" Julian asked looking at him searchingly.

"To know if anyone has been making any enquiries through you."

"No. Not yet, but the Italians do take longer over these things. Do you want to leave me your address and phone number and then I can let you know if I hear anything?"

"OK I will leave this with you" and Edward put a card down on the desk and began to leave. They shook hands and Julian noticed that Edward was looking quite worried. He couldn't help wondering what he knew about Andrea's death.

Edward was worried. He travelled all over the world raising money for development projects which were taking off in many parts of the world. He enjoyed watching it all happen and seeing the projects grow and his clients get richer and there never seemed to be any danger in the work. People just did not get killed. It must be something else that Andrea was in. The commission rates paid to Edward were very good so he was able to live at a very good rate and stay in all the best hotels wherever he went. He was married to a quiet reserved English woman who looked after him well and their two children who were now away at university. He had made many friends in the property investment business and he was able to take his family on long holidays to any of the lovely islands in the Caribbean as he had established a second home there where they spent most of the winter. He had his own boat and a houseboy who looked after everything when he went back to England. He had many clients in England who had invested in one or other of his projects and they had never had any problems, so what was different about investors in Rome, or was there no connection between Andrea's death and his investment with Edward?

Edward chose his ties carefully and the next morning he was dressing in front of the bedroom mirror to be as well dressed as usual.

"I think I should go back to Rome to see if I can help with any enquiries." He was saying to his wife.

"Oh don't be daft!" she replied firmly, "What is it to do with you? You weren't even that close! And anyway, if you appeared on the scene the Italian police would believe that you were involved in some way. Don't even think about it!" And that was the end of the matter.

CHAPTER SIX

The construction industry was not doing so well and the large companies were beginning to pull in their belts and cut overheads, so Julian realised that the legal department would have to follow suit and reduce in numbers. His private legal work had overtaken his company work now, so he should be one of the first to leave, so he gave in his notice and just took his work home. It was such a big step but just seemed to go so smoothly. He hardly noticed that one day he was driving to work and the next day he was simply doing the same work in his dining room at home.

Where the clients came from he never really knew, but they kept on ringing and making appointments to see him. Some were friends of friends and others had been recommended by old clients. It seemed that everyone had a problem and needed a lawyer, and he would never turn anyone away unless he felt that they did not actually have any case at all. That was very rare. He worked away and always made sure that he answered every letter he received on the same day. Julian was as efficient as he was caring. Sometimes the complexity of a case could be too much for him as he could hardly be an expert at everything, but then he was so thankful that the English legal system has two tiers and he only had to send papers on any difficult matter to counsel for a specialist's opinion. Nobody was left on the shelf and he never believed in specialisation. He had qualified by taking detailed examinations in fifteen different areas of law and that is what he would cover in his work. When asked if he did specialise—as this was becoming normal in big city firms—he would always reply that he tried to avoid cases concerning "collisions of ships at sea" or "space travel".

His favourite clients were those who put complete faith in him and therefore told him everything. There is nothing worse than half a story, as Julian soon discovered in litigation work that if his own client did not tell him the whole truths, the other side would soon discover it and probably win their case as a result. Like Diana who was rather scatty and told Julian that she had been involved in a collision in her car and had been charged with driving without due care and attention. She told him quite shyly that she had only collided with one lorry, but when Julian arrived at the Magistrates' Court he found that the police had called five witnesses to give evidence that they had seen Diana's car collide with the lorry and then swerve into a second car and bounce off that onto a third car! She was lucky that no one was injured, so Julian was able to argue in her favour to the best of his ability that she had merely lost concentration for a brief moment with tragic consequences, and she got off lightly with a small fine.

Julian had got used to working from home with just one secretary, and all his clients seemed to like that as they knew who was dealing with their case and that it was not being fobbed off onto some student lawyer to mess up. He enjoyed his meetings with clients and often became a part of their business dealings.

Hassan was one client who was cunning enough during the period of property price increases to realise that by making friends with a surveyor who worked for a particular Building Society, he could borrow more money with a mortgage advanced by them on the basis of the surveyor's exaggerated valuation to buy a property than it actually cost. He would then sell the property at a profit and make a lot of money without having invested anything to buy it in the first place. Julian acted for Hassan and believed that he had the right to depend on the surveyor's valuation and was not made aware of the actual purchase price agreed between Hassan and his seller until he was instructed to exchange contracts. Then he saw that the valuation was higher than the purchase price, but that was not uncommon, and anyway the surveyor was employed by the Building Society so Julian saw that as their problem and not his.

The trouble came when the property market slumped rapidly and Hassan could not sell his flat at a profit and he had not saved enough money to settle with the Building Society. They soon discovered what had been going on and decided to sue Julian for their loss as they had to sell the property for less money than they had lent to Hassan. He had after all been instrumental in the transaction and they had to try to recover their money from someone! Julian immediately informed his insurers who took the matter up with the Law Society who made the final decision with regard to settlement of the claim. They wrote to Julian accusing him of unprofessional conduct and he replied insisting that he had merely taken instructions from a client.

Julian's professional indemnity insurance policy protected him financially, and the insurance company stopped the case by negotiating terms of settlement with the Building Society, but Julian was furious because that meant that he was considered to have been guilty of defrauding the Building Society when the entire matter was nothing to do with him at all. Now there was a black mark against his name in the Law Society. It would not be the last.

Martin was a nasty piece of work and Julian mistrusted him on sight, but he was only asking for Julian to help because his brother had died intestate leaving an infant daughter. That went well and Julian set up a trust for the daughter and liaised with the mother, but it soon came to his notice that Martin was living in his brother's council flat and pretending to be the brother. Julian wrote to the brother informing him of the error of his ways and warning him that the local authority would soon be commencing action against him unless he vacated the flat. Martin was furious at being caught out and when he did hear from the local authority as Julian had predicted he was so angry that he wrote to the Law Society with a pack of lies about Julian and how he had cheated him and acted unprofessionally. It was all made up and the stories he told were either untrue or distorted, but the department of the Law Society dealing with such complaints followed it through by sending a representative to visit Julian and discuss the matter. They were suspicious and evidently followed up all complaints made against sole practitioners. It seemed that most of the compensation payments which had been made to clients by the Solicitors' Indemnity Fund for solicitors' negligence had been made against sole practitioners, so the Law Society was getting nervous about any such complaints and now always followed them up.

Julian could tell at once that Clarence was a homosexual with a chip on his shoulder about something—probably he had failed the Law Society's exam and could not be admitted as a solicitor, so he got a job working in the policing unit instead. Anyway he was devious with his questions and somehow failed to grasp the simplicity of the evidence in the letters which were being shown to him. Julian had come across his type before in clerks at various courts and elsewhere on the periphery of the profession pretending to be lawyers, but always angry inside knowing that they never would be. So he told the full story of how Martin had tried to cheat the local authority by not telling them about his brother's death. He thought he could just move in and take over his brother's council flat without even thinking that the same local authority would be issuing his brother's Death Certificate. When he was challenged, he tried to blame Julian, but without avail since Julian had all his files of letters to back up the truth of the matter.

The meeting was a disaster even though Julian tried to be friendly in his usual way as he had no feelings of guilt, and showed him all the relevant copy letters, but he could tell that Clarence still didn't believe him and just sat there making notes which would go on Julian's file about his feelings regarding the matter. Julian was not given any details about these, but he guessed that everything would come to the surface later. A few weeks went by before a formal letter arrived from the Law Society virtually telling him that they did not believe or disbelieve his story, but that they would only erase the complaint from his record if it was formally withdrawn by Martin.

Julian knew that letters from the Law Society were copied to both sides, so Martin would also have received a copy of the same letter. He was therefore not surprised to receive a telephone call from Martin asking for a meeting on neutral ground. Julian suggested that they meet in the bar of a local big hotel where there would be a lot of people around and Martin agreed. Julian was sure that Martin wanted to try a little blackmail and ask him for money to formally withdraw his villainous complaint, so he promptly telephoned his old client Peter to ask whether he could spare a couple of his team to come and be silent witnesses to the meeting. He was only too pleased to oblige and the meeting was set.

Martin strode into the hotel lounge looking as though he had everything under control and had even brought a witness of his own. Julian asked them to share a drinks table with him near the bar. Peter's friends were only two tables away and well able to hear everything that was said but did not give away the fact that they were listening to everything. Julian opened the conversation by telling Martin that his false complaint had got him nowhere, and to close the matter he should write another letter to the Law Society withdrawing his complaint.

Martin smiled and said that he had that in mind but it would cost Julian a lot of money, so Julian asked how much and warned Martin that he was engaging in blackmail—which he regarded as particularly wicked when both parties knew that the basic facts were untrue. Martin stood up when he realised that Julian had no intention of paying him and immediately before he could get away Julian called across to his friends listening at the other table.

"Did you hear all of that?" he asked loudly and pointedly.

Martin stood perfectly still and his face went white. His friend was running for the door. He clearly did not want to be implicated and for all he knew these other men were from the police.

"Yes, we got it all!" said one of them, looking down at his notebook.

"You better think again!" Julian shouted to Martin who was already making for the door.

Nothing more was heard from the Law Society and Julian never heard from Martin again, but he was learning that such incidents built up against a man's professional record whether true or false, and he was becoming angry about a system he would never be able to change.

CHAPTER SEVEN

The practice was doing well and Julian was enjoying his work. He changed his secretary from time to time when one moved on for personal reasons, but he always found that there was a massive demand for jobs like he was offering of a "one to one" kind. It took him a few years to realise that deep down so many of them were looking for their "Mr Right" to walk through that door.

Janet was one of the best typists that he had ever employed and she could cheerfully type a letter listening to her dictation machine and having a conversation with Julian about a completely different matter at the same time. She was a joy for him to have around, but Julian never "dipped his pen into the Company ink" as they say, so there was never any hanky panky or even a suggestion that they should have any kind of relationship other than as boss and secretary. She was a young good looking girl and enjoyed the closeness of working for one man who recognised this without ever making a pass at her.

It came as quite a surprise to Julian when Harry, who was one of Julian's favourite divorce clients asked if he could bring Janet as his partner to one of Julian's Henley Regatta parties. Once Julian had recovered from the shock he was quite pleased to have been the instigator of such a relationship. He wondered how long it would last, but in the meanwhile they all became quite a close family exchanging visits to each other's houses and meeting each other's friends.

They married eventually and the marriage lasted for some years before the age difference began to show and they grew apart. Divorce was unavoidable and Julian had to decide which side he was on. Harry had always been his client so he asked him if the divorce would be entirely amicable. He assured him that it was and it transpired that his financial offer was so generous that Janet knew that she would have been stupid to oppose it and so the deal was done.

Julian worried that the proposed settlement was too generous and that Harry may blame him in years to come for not stopping the payment. He did not want to lose Harry's friendship so Julian arranged for Harry to sign a document agreeing that the payment was entirely his own choice and against his lawyer's advice. Harry could not resist adding a clause to the document to the effect that Julian should also agree that any other ladies he introduced to Harry should be self-supporting!

Harry had a very successful business of his own employing over a hundred people in North London, but he agreed with Julian that he would rather have a lawyer on a personal basis than go to one of those large city firms where they were always farming cases out to students and paralegals who knew nothing about the client personally, even though the partner in charge pretended to be running the case. They always got the big litigation cases—and charged the monstrous fees—but Julian had never been greedy so he was rather pleased that he was never asked to take on such cases as the paperwork under the new practice rules and regulations made it almost impossible for a sole practitioner to cope with the work involved.

Julian was over sixty years old but he never felt his age, and could have gone on for years while his clients kept on coming to him for advice, but one day he received a shock which changed his entire attitude. The Law Society wrote to him to say that in view of the small complaints which had been passed to them over the years (none of which had come to any fruition or even become serious disciplinary matters) Julian's practicing certificate would only be renewed on the basis that he continued to practice in partnership with another solicitor or in a firm of solicitors. He was furious as there was no one to speak to or challenge about the decision which had been made entirely behind his back without any consultation. Who could he turn to? He did not want to take on a partner or apply for a job with a larger firm at his age, so he went to speak to one of his old legal buddies who quickly drew his attention to the fact that solicitors have one huge advantage over other members of the public in that they are entitled to petition the Master of the Rolls for a hearing of any complaint whatsoever against the Law Society.

Julian couldn't wait, and he promptly notified the Law Society that unless they withdrew their limitation on his practice he would be applying for such a hearing. Well of course organisations like the Law Society do not engage in about-turns, so after receiving their reply to this effect, Julian started to prepare his papers for the High Court applying to the most senior judge in the land to hear his complaint.

It was all quite exciting really as he was past the usual retirement age anyway and had been advised by his accountant that his savings were quite adequate to keep him "in the manner to which he had become accustomed", but he knew that in his heart of hearts his anger was over a matter of principle. He was not going to just let some junior clerk in the Law Society put some papers in front of his boss and request that a sole practitioner should not be allowed to continue with his career when there had been absolutely no legitimate complaints made against him by any client. He knew very well that this was just a clash of personalities with that Clarence character who couldn't have made his feelings more obvious. Julian had already written to the President of the Law Society to make this point, but he had only received a very smarmy reply and had never been asked to attend a consultation with anyone in authority to discuss the position. This had simply become a matter of the large organisation squashing an unimportant junior member. It could never have happened to the partner of a large city firm.

The Master of the Rolls had obviously read all the documents scrupulously as he asked Julian only very pertinent questions and then gave his judgment in a very fair way. The Law Society were fully empowered by statute to declare whatever restrictions they wished upon its members and could admit and curtail any solicitor's practice, he said. He had read all of Julian's papers and sympathised with him, but in the end it was for the organisation to make its own decisions. Julian was overjoyed to see him then turn to the solicitor acting for the Law Society and declare in a very meaningful way that with such strong powers he hoped that the Law Society would use them carefully and fairly but in this case he had decided that he had no power to intervene. So that was the end of the matter and Julian had to decide whether to continue in practice as ordained by them or to retire.

Cyril had been a friend of Julian's for many years even though he had been struck off the roll of solicitors for some years because of his involvement in some financial scandal. It hadn't bothered him though because he knew that he could continue to help people and just go to a friendly solicitor like Julian if he ever needed to use someone with a practicing certificate. The Law Society didn't like it but there wasn't much they could do providing Cyril didn't overstep the mark and pretend that he was authorised by them. So now the tide had turned, and whereas Julian thought he was going into retirement, in fact many old clients continued to come to him and they just laughed when he told them that he was not authorised to practice. They needed his help and did not care about the Law Society and, like Cyril, Julian simply did not overstep the mark and engage in litigation or ever sign his name as a practicing solicitor.

Wendy had used Julian as her solicitor many years before when she had bought her little flat in Fulham, and now she wanted to sell it and came back to him to act for her in the transaction. He explained his new position to her and then told her that actually she did not need a solicitor at all as she could act for herself. It was her flat and she could sell it how and to whom she liked. This pleased her but the buyer's solicitors were angry as they could not make any threats or demands against someone who they could not report to the Law Society over the negotiations if they became difficult, but Julian soon found that this weighed heavily in his favour and to the advantage of his client. Why had he not thought of it before when talking to Cyril? He was a free man and could actually be of more use to a client in negotiations than a practicing solicitor who was bound by so many silly rules and regulations.

There was no need to worry about indemnity insurance now as he simply told anyone who came to him for advice that he was not insured. They didn't care as they had no intention of suing their lawyer anyway. Anyone who did so was a special kind of client and Julian was happy to say that he had never had to deal with such people. Only the Building Society who had tried to claim their losses from him had gone anywhere near that, and he was well rid of it.

Julian always used to open his mail with a kind of foreboding as to its contents relating to cases he was handling, but now all that stopped as he was impervious to other solicitors throwing practice regulations at him, and he suddenly realised how the profession had changed since he was first admitted all those thirty years before. Now solicitors were scoring points off each other rather than playing straight with their cases. He was well out of it, but so very pleased that he could continue to help his friends. He knew the law and that mattered. He was a happy man.

THE END

Barry's Boarders

CHAPTER ONE

Stephen had always thought that he should be a company man rather than a loner, but that was probably because he had been brought up in boarding schools and always been surrounded by other boys and learned all about team spirit. When he left school he had immediately been called up to do his National Service for two years, but when he was commissioned as an officer he signed on for a Short Service Commission to serve an extra three years in the British Army. So he had enjoyed his time travelling from one military unit to another in the Far East. He was always surrounded by many people of different nationalities and found it easy to get on with them. He was not yet twenty one years old, but grown up for his age as he had been left very much alone by his parents at holiday times as a boy, so he knew how to take care of himself.

When he returned to England as a civilian he qualified as a solicitor and worked for several large companies. A few of the people he worked with were a bit jealous of him, probably because he was a good mixer and did not show the kind of shyness that most Englishmen do. He just went straight into a problem head-on and tried to solve it head on without fear. But then he could easily rub people up the wrong way, especially if they disagreed with him—which was often the case as most legal problems do have two sides. He did not believe much in diplomacy, as he thought this was so often an excuse for weakness, and he liked to call a spade a spade and to get on with whatever he thought was the right thing to do.

He worked for an international Insurance Company for five years, and although he got on very well with most of his colleagues, some of them did not appreciate his open manner in conferences and board meetings which sometimes put them down even if it achieved results. That would often just make matters worse as someone was then going to be shown up as being wrong. It was different if he was dealing with a personal legal matter as then he tried his best to win the argument on their behalf and of course they liked that.

The time came with a downturn in the national economy when the company needed to make severe cuts in its staff, and Stephen decided that he should move on, and while he was looking around for a suitable position, he did not waste his time but continued to help many of his personal friends who came to him for legal assistance—and their friends who were referred to him. He was working from home, but as a very social man he continued to frequent the popular bars and clubs in his part of London in the evenings after his work, and always found that he was being introduced to new people who had legal problems that needed his assistance.

Without even realising it, Stephen had started a successful private practice dealing with one case after another, and while he recognised that his principle job was to help people who were in trouble, his favourite clients were those who knew exactly what they wanted and looked to him for legal assistance when this was required. He did not approve of legal specialisation, as that had not been the way he was taught in Law School where English Law had been divided into fifteen different subjects and if any student failed in any one subject that would bar him from being admitted as a solicitor, so he always believed that he should use all his knowledge and not just parts of it. There were many he met who were brilliant on all the legal subjects but just could not grasp Accounts which was one of the compulsory exams. So they were turned away from the profession which he thought was unfair after years of study. Stephen was not afraid of figures, and he had learned the secret from one of his clever student friends that in the exams it didn't matter if you got the correct result as long as you appeared to know what you were doing in the calculation. They must have been right because he passed.

Stephen kept his solicitor's practice going for many years in his small office near Bond Street and he was happy to notice that the volume of work always stayed about the same, as did his income, as he did not relish the thought of a large practice which he could not handle alone. Many of his legal friends in the West End worked hard to enlarge their practices when they then had to take on more staff and move premises to be able to accommodate them. That was happening even more in the City where the number of partners in a good firm would increase well into the hundreds, and of course many members of the staff never met many others. This meant that clients were passed from one partner to another depending on the type of legal problem and they all convinced each other that if they only did one kind of work then they must be good at it. Stephen disagreed and stayed put as a general practitioner who was always willing to help a client with any legal problem, and if it fell outside his scope he would refer the matter to a specialist counsel for his opinion. It never failed, and as a result he kept many clients for years as they had no reason to go elsewhere.

The lease of his office was coming to an end so he asked his bank manager for a loan to acquire a new lease either for the same premises or another office nearby. Peter Black had enjoyed being Stephen's bank manager and had passed many clients to him, but he was surprised at the request.

"Why do you need new premises at all?" he asked. "I mean the clients come to see you and not some swanky office don't they?"

Stephen did not quite follow the point, so he asked Peter to explain.

"Well I know your flat in Chelsea well enough after all the times you have so kindly invited me there, and as far as I can see it would be ideal for running a private practice. Perhaps you didn't realise that your clients come to see you and not the office!"

The point had not dawned on Stephen until then, but he suddenly realised how right Peter was, and that he could so easily turn his sitting room around to be a very comfortable office and far less noisy than being adjacent to a busy shopping street. So he moved his office into his flat and continued his practice from there.

CHAPTER TWO

Twenty years went by with Stephen continuing to work in the same happy way always with his one secretary who enjoyed the privacy and almost intimacy of looking after one man and being involved in so many interesting matters. Stephen never thought of retiring as he enjoyed the work so much, but his accountant had advised him to make regular payments into a retirement savings plan, so that had just become one of the normal items of expenditure.

One of his new clients who had been referred to him was Barry Parsons who had come down to the big city from Newcastle with a business plan but he needed legal assistance. He was a good looking young man of about twenty five years who had tried many different jobs in the north and had eventually decided that he would move south to the London area where the money was. He had that strong Geordie accent which many found endearing and he believed in being straightforward and honest.

Barry told Stephen that he strongly believed that there was a huge market for cheap tourist accommodation in London as hundreds of youngsters were arriving at the various train stations and airports to visit London every day without having made any arrangements for their accommodation. He had discovered that there were numerous residential buildings in the most popular parts of the capital to let for a rent which was well below the total amount which he knew would be paid by all the student travellers he could pack into them. The individual rents paid by the students was always way below the market rent for cheap hotel accommodation so everyone was happy. There was no question of any capital sum being involved in taking over the accommodation, as the landlords only asked for a small deposit to be paid in advance and then a weekly or monthly rent on a regular basis. He would then sign a Tenancy Agreement which he first wanted to clear with Stephen who would check that there were no conditions in it which would prevent or hinder Barry's hostel business. It was soon agreed that this should be done in the name of a different limited company for each hostel. The ideas was that if any of them got into difficulties, that company would cease to trade without affecting the other hostels which were run under different company names. This seemed to be a sensible idea to everybody.

Barry had a team of supporters who combed the chosen areas of London near the West End to find suitable premises which were large enough to take sufficient beds to make it worth while to take over and convert into a hostel. Barry then moved in with all his old furniture and equipment to house all those many travellers he had collected from the railway stations with those rucksacks on their backs.

There were numerous legal problems concerning the hostels which were always in a residential area. The neighbours did not appreciate the noise of late night revellers, and often complained to the Local Authority. There were also cases where the lease of the premises contained restrictions with regard to the number of residents permitted which Barry always ignored to maximise his profits. The Local Authority were also on the look-out for breaches in local bye-laws appertaining to properties in multiple occupation, fire regulations and other matters which they were quick to write to Barry about. He was strong enough to ride rough-shod over the many complaints, and just passed them to Stephen when any such warning letters or serious Notices arrived on his desk.

Barry was keeping Stephen very busy with all these problems, but what surprised Stephen was that Barry had absolutely no idea of how to keep accounts, and if there had not been such a healthy gap between the income from his "back-packers" and expenditure in running his hostels, he would undoubtedly have become bankrupt very quickly. As it was, the business flourished and went from strength to strength with more and more hostels being taken over and let out to so many young foreign holiday-makers and students.

Very few houses or flats let out on short leases stipulated the maximum number of people allowed to occupy the premises, or whether or not they could be used as hostel accommodation, so it was usually a matter for the Local Authority to make a fuss on health grounds if there was a complaint that a certain building or flat was over populated. Such cases were always referred to Stephen who supported the business and usually arrange for some kind of compromise to be agreed. Barry was never told to move on and was never taken to Court. The officials in the Local Authority wanted to do their job, but were usually too timid to actually take a case to Court or cause any major problem by issuing demands or warrants. So Barry continued to operate near the limit, but that was the essence of the business to take in as many back-packers as possible to increase his profits.

Barry was running a strictly cash business, as he took on new Tenancy Agreements for new properties in different names but never opened any bank accounts for any of the companies which he quoted to the relevant authorities as being responsible for those properties which he was rapidly turning into hostels. He was just taking cash payments from his lodgers every week and then paying all his bills in cash. Sometimes when he received a really large bill for local authority rates or council tax he would go to Stephen with cap in hand and ask for a personal loan to pay that bill—which he then repaid in cash with handsome interest on a weekly basis.

There were very few maintenance or staffing problems with Barry's business because so many of his lodgers wanted to help with anything they could, and they fiercely protected any quasi position they had been given on the staff. Most of them were impecunious students from one of the Commonwealth countries and after a few weeks in London often decided that they wanted to stay. This often presented legal problems which Stephen was happy to help with, so if he needed any maintenance or decorative works doing to his house, he only had to say the word and there would be a team of young keen volunteers on his doorstep. By the same token if any of the lodgers had a legal problem, Barry would simply take them over to Stephen's office for the matter to be dealt with.

Barry had two partners to help him with the business. One was his younger brother Alan, a pleasant quiet man with an even stronger north country dialect than his brother, and the other was Samuel who originated in Sydney, Australia, and was always insisting that he intended going back there. Barry didn't believe that he would ever leave London but Stephen did, as Sam was always talking to him about "back home" and making it clear that he was investing in a similar letting business in Sydney which was being run by his family there while he was in London.

Sam had a magical charm like so many young Australians, and he was always able to fill the company van with back-packers he found every time he went to Victoria station, no matter what time of day or night, and deliver them to one or other of the company hostels which had the most bed spaces available. It seemed that there was an inexhaustible supply of lodgers whenever the company needed to fill any of its spaces, so the cash flow was excellent.

One day an official from British Rail stopped Sam on Victoria Station and asked for a meeting with representatives of the company to discuss the matter of passengers being stopped on railway platforms. Barry insisted that this should take place in his solicitor's office. It soon came to light that the only complaint had originated from a competitor who was also trying to fill their hostel accommodation, so when Stephen realised this, he made sure that the matter was speedily dropped and never raised again.

CHAPTER THREE

Barry's next venture was to take a lease of a pub in Chelsea. At first this seemed to be totally disconnected from his hostel business and rather a wild scheme for him to undertake as no accommodation was included, but Barry was married to a French wife who adored anything to do with food and needed something to do. Stephen negotiated the terms of the pub Lease for her, and soon she was hiring excellent chefs who were producing top quality lunches. The pub became very popular and was full every day. Barry was a kind hearted man and to show his appreciation for all Stephen's work for his businesses with all the small problems which cropped up, he thought it would be a pleasant ritual for them all to have lunch together in the new French Restaurant on a weekly basis by way of a Company Board Meeting. Stephen's secretary was also invited to go along, so it became a kind of weekly business lunch party. It worked very well as the food was good and the ambiance perfect for informal chats about the large or small problems being faced by any parts of Barry's business ventures.

Barry was always honest and even proud of his modest background and upbringing, but his lack of business experience soon began to show when he had to prepare various company accounts for Companies House or the Inland Revenue when he just seemed to fight shy of producing these and hated to even discuss figures at all. Everything else in the business seemed to be running well, so Stephen never pressed him on the point, and thought that if things went really badly for Barry at any time over his tax affairs, he would be sure to bring him any threatening letters from the Revenue or the VAT authorities, but no such letters were ever brought to him so Stephen thought no more about it. He did think that it was rather strange that Barry never showed him any profit and loss accounts, but he had got used to the fact that this was an area of Barry's business that was private to him and really none of his business as he was strictly the Company lawyer—which did not include being their accountant—if they even had one.

Stephen got used to Barry's visits to his office on almost a weekly basis, especially when he owed him money as Barry was meticulous about repaying his loans with interest, as he had a very high standard of morals. He probably also appreciated that if he defaulted with his repayments then his source of regular loans could be brought to a halt. That was not going to happen, and for his part Stephen was pleased to continue making the loans, as this tied him into the business, and Barry would not be taking his legal work to another lawyer while the partnership continued in such a satisfactory way.

Inevitably the hostel accommodation business grew larger, and Barry had at least six different properties under his belt being managed by him together with his partners. He formed a new limited company to manage each property, so he was declaring each of them to be a new business for tax reasons, and was putting off the day when he would have to produce accounts to the Inland Revenue.

In fact the axe fell on him from a completely different direction which no one saw coming. He had formed a kind of loose partnership with a rich Arab who was very impressed with his business, and rather than opening up in opposition by starting his own business, Faisal agreed to pay the necessary finance for Barry to take over a huge fifteen storey building which was originally an abandoned old college which had closed down and lay empty in West Kensington. The Local Authority were glad to find a taker for the huge eyesore of a property which was beginning to attract tramps and the walls of the ground floor of the building were already covered in graffiti.

Barry took the project under his belt with his usual efficiency by just appointing new members of his growing team from very willing new immigrant back-packers who learned very quickly all that was required of them. The location could not have been better, and the freeholders were delighted to have found a tenant on whom they imposed very few restrictions. All they wanted was for their building to be cleaned up and looked after and their monthly rent paid. The amount sounded exorbitant to Faisal until he compared it with the rents which would be paid for the huge number of bed spaces which would be let out to back packers. Barry took it all in his stride and had the place cleaned up and running within a very short time, and he soon enlarged the business to provide canteen catering and indoor sports facilities. He was a natural organizer and the members of his staff adored him.

Then one day one of the lifts stopped working. The second lift was not particularly reliable either, so when the news spread around, all those rooms above the third and fourth floors became very unpopular and almost impossible to let. Complaints were pouring into Barry and he contacted the landlords to ask them to see to the lifts, but an argument soon ensued as to who was responsible for attending to the maintenance of the lifts. Barry brought the matter to Stephen who immediately advised him that it was for the landlords to keep the lifts in working order and Barry should chase them to put the work in hand. Nothing was being done and the upper rooms were remaining empty. Stephen supported him as far as he could by writing to the landlords and their solicitors, but all to no avail as the landlords were having an argument with the company who had installed the lifts as to whether they were liable under the guarantee they had given some years ago with regard to the on-going maintenance of the lifts.

The income from the building reduced drastically when no one wanted to move into any of the upper rooms. Faisal was furious and stopped paying any rent to the landlords who promptly issued a legal notice, so Barry went to see Stephen to ask his advice. Stephen warned him that he may well have a case against the landlords to see to the lifts, but in accordance with the terms of his lease he was duty bound to continue paying the rent and should wait until the matter of the lifts was resolved before he could make any claim against the landlords for his losses. Faisal would have none of it and just refused to pay the rent. He just insisted that he was in the business to reap profits and not to pay rents with no profit and he would not listen to Stephen. Barry hated the impasse as he was not an argumentative man, but he did not have the kind of money required to pay the rent while there was no income, and while Stephen was prepared to lend him the occasional hundred or two hundred pounds, he could see that this dispute was going to continue for a long time and the debt increase to thousands of pounds before it was resolved. So he could not help Barry with a loan on this occasion.

The arguments continued, and instead of the landlords expediting their action with the lift company to resolve the dispute and getting them fixed, they turned their attention onto Barry and his company to demand payment of the outstanding rent which was growing bigger every week. There was a clause in the Lease authorising them to terminate the Lease in the event of non-payment of the rent after twenty one days, and as this time had now expired, they made an application to the Court for an eviction order to be made and for the building to be returned to them.

There was a lot at stake for Barry, as he did not keep that kind of money available, and his business partner Faisal was washing his hands of the whole business which he was convinced was wrong. He had never taken legal advice and firmly believed that the landlords were wicked regardless of whatever Stephen told him. So he wanted the matter to go to Court as he was sure that he would win. Stephen was not so sure, but he had no alternative but to defend the action for Barry as the landlords were the Claimants and were looking for their rent and the return of the building.

Faisal had paid Stephen enough legal fees in advance to enable him to instruct Counsel to take the case, but as soon as the clerk to Counsel's chambers saw the amounts of money involved, he strongly advised Stephen to instruct a Q.C. to take the case. Stephen always advised his clients to take Counsel's advice, so the matter was passed to John Foulkes Q.C. who asked for an immediate conference. Faisal together with Barry and one of his managers all went with Stephen to Counsel's chambers in Lincoln's Inn where they sat around the large table in the conference room to discuss the matter with the QC together with his junior.

Reams of documents were produced mainly by Stephen to show Foulkes the full background of the story, and he took them over to turn them into an affidavit to serve on the other side the following day. He could see that Stephen was a sole practitioner, and when he heard that he only had one secretary he realised that most of the typing work would have to be done by his own typists in chambers. What was worse, was the fact that regardless of the contractual position between the lift company and the landlords, Foulkes seemed to be saying from the start that the rent should have been paid in accordance with the terms of the Lease and that his clients were wrong to withhold this. Nevertheless he proceeded with his defence at the hearing which had been set down by the landlords' solicitors in one of the Courts in the High Court in the Strand.

Stephen was sitting just behind Foulkes who had his junior sitting next to him and a pile of documents in front of him. He argued that the premises were not in the state in which they had been let to his client as they could not use the upper floors with the lifts not working properly, but his heart was not in the argument and it did not take the judge long to sum up the facts of the case. Barry had taken on a lease of premises under which he had to pay the rent under any circumstances, and whatever other claims he may have against the landlords they had reserved the right in the lease to terminate it in the event of the rent not being paid for twenty one days so that was that. All costs in the case to be paid by the Defendant.

The problem now was that Barry did not have the money to pay what was already owed, and then there was also a matter of the legal costs which had grown profusely over the few days the case had been managed by Foulkes QC. His clerk thought that he had a rich client on his hands and was horrified to hear that the cupboard was bare after the first payment had been made to him on account to instruct the QC in the first place. The barrister for the landlords was equally anxious for his clients to be paid not only what was due to them for the unpaid rent under the judgment, but also to enable them to meet his very high legal costs, so the action began to turn in different directions as he endeavoured to find whatever money there was in other companies which could be proved to be associated with the company which had taken over the disused college.

Then there was the matter of Stephen's participation in being the company secretary for those companies—and his knowledge of their internal affairs and the accounts of those companies. It was looking very black for all those concerned as the barristers on both sides were looking for any pot of gold to pay their fees which were now far greater than the sum owed the claimant landlord company. New affidavits were arriving at Stephen's address which had been drawn up by the solicitors for the landlords and delivered to his own counsel's chambers, but nothing was being drawn up by his own counsel to rebut any of the serious allegations made in those affidavits. The solicitors had evidently discovered that none of Barry's family or staff had any money and that they really did operate the business on a strictly cash basis with no money in the bank. There was therefore only one course of action open to them and that was to implicate their lawyer who was bound to have sufficient assets to be able to pay the amount being looked for. He may have to borrow from his bank or even sell his house, but a solicitor in private practice in Chelsea should be able to raise that kind of money.

As soon as Stephen saw which way the action was going he dismissed his QC and informed his clerk that he would be making a complaint to the Bar Council. There were careers at stake here and he could see that he was up against a stronger adversary. He had been there before and knew what he had to do. First he called Barry and asked him to bring in his partners Alan and Sam. They were all very shocked by the whole affair as they had seen the fight as being simply one over the lifts and a deferment of the rents due, and could hardly believe the terrible fact that everyone was being thrown out of the college building.

They were not going to be given the building back, so there was no point in trying to raise the overdue unpaid rent, or even their own barrister's fees, but if they did not pay the amount awarded by the Court to the opposing solicitors, then they would be taking action against Stephen to pay this amount. Stephen made it clear that if any action was taken against him personally then he would make all the partners co-defendants and it would all be very messy—and kill their friendship. Barry and Alan were nonplussed by the whole business, but Stephen could see that Sam understood perfectly and asked him to consider the position and find ways to raise the money required.

The barristers had been very thorough in their investigation into the business as they were looking for heavy payments to be made to them for their exaggerated fees. These were aimed at Stephen as he was responsible for instructing them, but of course it was the hostel team who were really liable if they could not get their Arabic partner Faisal to pay up for all the financial damage he had caused. All the various hostels had been brought into the claim for fees, as it had been a simple matter for the barristers to search Companies House for all the companies which Barry and his family had an interest, and to request the judge to incorporate all of them into the overall claim.

Sam saved the day by paying the full amount due to settle the case as ordered by the Court. This comprised the outstanding rent for the building and the landlords' complete legal costs. It remained for him to press his own partners and friends to repay him somehow.

CHAPTER FOUR

Barry had no assets to fall back on so it did not take Sam and his partners long to turn on him and make him bankrupt. They wanted their money back so they turned on the boss. He had to sell his house and then try to find a job. The case had ruined them all and their hostel business just vaporized. Sam disappeared after that and probably went to Australia as he had always promised to do. None of the partners had really understood the seriousness of the case, and Stephen was still being pressed to pay his own counsel's fees. He felt very strongly that these were exaggerated and should not be paid. Mr Foulkes had looked thoroughly into the case to take it into Court, but he had not checked on the true financial position of his clients' partnership the way the opposition had done, so now his clerk was trying to claim the amount from the solicitor who had instructed him. In fact he knew that Stephen had asked for a junior counsel but he had pressed him into taking a QC.

It was always a rule of the profession that a barrister cannot sue for his fees, so while Stephen fully intended only paying out what had been paid to him by his client, he knew that this could result in him being reported to the Law Society who had the power to refuse to grant him the renewal of his practicing certificate at the end of the year. He waited to see what would happen. He did not believe that the barristers were so greedy that they would actually see a solicitor struck off the roll in their endeavour to claim fees which he had not been paid by his client. He was wrong as the barristers' chambers persisted with their claim and never admitted that the failure of the case was entirely a result of their own incompetence.

Stephen was so upset by the whole episode that he was determined that the barristers involved should not be paid any more, and when the time came he deliberately did not apply for the renewal of his practicing certificate. He continued to help his friends as a consultant and was surprised to find that his clients and the general public were so ignorant of the rules of the legal profession that they really did not care whether he had a practicing certificate or not. He would of course be barred from taking cases into Court, but at his age he did not intend to continue with any litigation work anyway, so that was no loss.

At last he was free and suddenly he had no rules to curtail his activities. He felt free to criticize bad solicitors with the knowledge that he would no longer worry about the threat of being reported to the Law Society. His work diminished slightly simply because he wanted it to.

Barry was the only one to lose out badly by being made bankrupt and having to sell his home, but he was such a calm man in the face of total destruction that even when he had lost everything and was penniless, he admitted to Stephen that now he should start to take some courses in business activities and perhaps learn how to keep accounts. A man with his qualities was bound to rise again.

THE END

A Real Fiddle

CHAPTER ONE

Graham turned into the front doors of the hospital without even looking where he was going as he knew his way so well. At first he had been so impressed by the building as it was so different from the hospitals he remembered from years before with their long inhospitable corridors and serious looking nurses running round in fear of their ward sisters. Now everyone was so friendly and helpful, and visiting a patient was like meeting them in a top hotel. He came in every day at about the same day to see his brother Stephen and usually brought in some fruit or chocolate with the daily newspaper. He was very fond of Stephen and would do anything for him, but he had been told that the cancer was very serious and that he probably would not live very much longer. They had grown up together, but then Stephen had married that dreadful Helen woman and things had been very difficult as she didn't like Graham at all and even told him to stop visiting them at their home. Graham didn't mind as he didn't like her either.

That was all a few years ago, but then they had a daughter who they christened Victoria who was now nearly nine years old. The marriage had not gone at all well and eventually after years of arguing there was a messy divorce which resulted in little Vicky going to live with her mother. Stephen missed her very much, but he had paid enough money to Helen in the final divorce settlement to be sure that she would be able to look after Vicky without any financial worries. He just carried on living alone in his little suburban house and was pleased to be able to go and see his little Vicky every weekend. Helen didn't like that, but she knew that she had to comply with the Court Order enabling him to visit his daughter, and she was pleased that Stephen always brought something nice for Vicky.

Graham was very worried that his brother had not made a Will as he knew that Stephen had done quite well with his career and had probably invested in quite a profitable life insurance policy. He wanted to be sure that he would see a part of that when the worse came to the worse, and he was also concerned that Stephen had left money for their parents who were now very old and frail. Every time he raised the subject it seemed to annoy Stephen as he was a very superstitious man and truly believed that if he made a Will then it would hasten his end, and he was in no mood to do that. He had been enjoying life too much and he loved to see his daughter which he looked forward to every week when she came in to see him with her mother. He knew enough about the law to know that his daughter would get everything if he died and he was satisfied with that. Stephen knew that his brother Graham was a greedy boy and would rather cheat someone for sixpence than go and earn an honest shilling, so he had no intention of leaving anything to him.

Stephen was not looking so well, but Graham was always pleased to chat with him during his visits and talk about the family. Helen brought Vicky in to see him every two or three days when she was sure that Graham was not visiting, but the atmosphere was always strained between them because she was always trying to cut the visit short and take the child away. It was different with Graham, but still Stephen didn't like the pressure of his brother trying to get him to sign documents as though he wanted him to die and just leave him some money. That made him even more determined to just do nothing.

"Don't worry Graham—I'm just fine! Anyway, if anything happens to me I have looked after everything and left the papers in my office."

Graham winced as that meant that he would never know what arrangements his brother had made, and he would have to just wait and see. They carried on talking about good times and things Graham had been up to, but soon it was time for him to leave. He knew that his brother would not last much longer and he was very sad and even more upset that he had not been assured that he would be looked after financially.

A few days later Stephen died and Graham immediately made an appointment to see the local solicitor who was Barry Edwards who was a sole practitioner. He had run a private practice for over thirty years from an office in the High Street and worked with only one secretary Nancy, who knew all his clients and kept their files in her immaculate system. She had met Graham before when he had been in to see Barry about some property matter nearly two years before. She didn't like him then and she didn't like him now, but still she offered him a cup of coffee.

"Yes, I am quite sure that he didn't leave a Will" Graham replied to Barry's direct question. "I know because I kept asking him to make one in the hospital, but he told me that he didn't want to. He seemed to think that it would shorten his life!"

"Well in that case we will have to apply for Letters of Administration to be granted in favour of his next of kin. He divorced his wife and his daughter is too young, so will that be you?"

"Well no," Graham replied. "I think parents come before a brother don't they?"

"Yes. Quite correct. Can you ask them to come in and see me or should I send the documents to them for signature?"

"I'll see" replied Graham not quite sure of himself. "They are getting on a bit, so I must ask them if they want to come in. It may be a bit much for them, but I'll tell you what they say."

"OK" agreed Barry, "and if you give me their address now I will drop them a line to tell them about the documents I will need to see. Then of course there is the matter of the daughter. I understand that she is still under age and will therefore probably be represented by her mother. Can I have her address please as I will need to write to her. I take it she has been informed?"

"Oh yes. I gave her the bad news to pass on to the daughter," Graham replied as he jotted down the addresses for Barry.

"Well then nothing more that we can do today. Just let me know when you have received the Death Certificate and spoken to your parents about coming back in."

Barry stood up to open the door for Graham with a friendly smile and a handshake and watched him go. He wouldn't trust him with half a milk bar he was thinking, but that shouldn't matter in this case as the Court would appoint two Administrators who were not going to be opposed by any of the family. That would be decided in a small private hearing after all the relevant affidavits and documents had been filed in the Court.

CHAPTER TWO

"Helen Johnson on the telephone" Nancy whispered as she passed the handset to Barry who frowned trying to remember who that was.

"Stephen's widow!" she muttered in his ear, and he brightened up, suddenly on the ball.

"Hello Mrs Johnson!" he began cheerily. "I was sorry to hear about Stephen. How can I help you?

"Well I understand that his brother Graham has been in to see you and I wondered if you were acting for him as his solicitor or whether you will be acting for my ex-husband's Estate. As I am sure you know he had a daughter who lives with me."

Barry immediately grasped the significance of the question she was asking and put her at ease as quickly as he could to assure her that he would only advise Graham so far as Stephen's administrators instructed him to do so, and they had not even been appointed yet.

"Would you like me to apply to the Court for you to be appointed as one of the Administrators?" he asked.

"Oh I don't think Graham would like that!" she exclaimed. "Perhaps it would be better if the parents were appointed as I don't have any problems with them and they often come over to see Vicky."

"OK" Barry agreed. "They should be coming in to see me soon and I will let you know what they say. I am sure they will be pleased to have your backing."

A few days went by before Graham telephoned to make an appointment to come in again. Barry greeted him and was surprised to see that he was carrying an old violin case. Graham smiled and immediately began to explain.

"I have been searching around Stephen's house to make a list of his valuables and to see where he left all his documents and bank statements as I am sure you will need to see all those, and I came across this old violin in the attic!"

"Is there anything special about it?" Barry asked a little bewildered as to why it should be so important.

"Well I wondered that until I opened it and found this newspaper cutting inside."

He reached over and handed a yellowed old cutting to Barry who immediately saw that it was dated nearly two years before and he read it:-

"LOST STRADIVARI VIOLIN.

Yesterday several members of the Royal Philharmonic Orchestra were waiting for a bus outside the Albert Hall carrying their musical instruments, and when the bus arrived they got onto it but one of the musicians left a very valuable old violin lying on the pavement. He thought that another of his group had the violin and immediately returned to the bus stop only to find that it had gone.

The violin is one of only five in the world which was made in the 18th century by the famous Italian Stradivari family and is thought to be worth over a million pounds as the last one to be auctioned nearly reached that price in New York. The insurers are endeavoring to trace whoever picked up the violin which was still in its original case but they have not yet received any clues as to its whereabouts, but hope it will soon be returned."

Barry was aghast at the implication of the note and immediately opened the violin case. If he was looking down at a real Stradivari, it looked to him like any other old violin, but the cutting he had just read told him all he needed to know. He turned to Graham and asked him

"What do you expect me to do with it?"

"Well I thought it must be worth a few bob!" he replied with a sly smile. Then he handed Barry another scrap of paper which was apparently in Stephen's handwriting. It said simply:-

"To My Mum and Dad. I hope you can sell this for a good price and have the lolly you never had before! All my love Stephen."

Barry suddenly realised that the implication of the two notes had not occurred to Graham, who could only visualise selling the violin and reaping a huge reward for himself, so he set about telling him the true position.

"This is called "stealing by finding" and it never belonged to your brother," he explained. "You should return it to the true owner as quickly as possible as I am sure it is sadly missed!"

"Well I wouldn't know where to begin to find the owner," Graham replied very disappointed that Barry was not telling him that he was sitting on a fortune. Quite the reverse in fact. The implication was that if he did not return the violin to the true owner he could be in serious trouble.

"Can I leave it with you then?" he asked, clearly disappointed.

"If you like" Barry replied. "I can make a few enquiries and let you know how it goes."

Graham then handed over all the other papers and documents he had found in Stephen's house and left Barry to carry on with the application for administrators to be appointed to distribute Stephen's estate. He also left the violin.

As soon as Graham had left the office, Barry picked up the telephone and got through to Sotheby's Auction House. They had a special department dealing with musical instruments and the man in charge was very knowledgeable about missing valuable items and promised to visit Barry the following week.

The old violin case was propped up in the corner of Barry's office to await the visit and nobody gave it a second look. Legal offices are not prone to burglary as they do not often contain valuables of any kind or keep much petty cash as most legal transactions are carried out by way of instructions given to banks on the sale and purchase of properties, but by pure chance Barry's office was burgled that week. The office door was forced open and the lock broken, but the thieves only took the petty cash box containing a few pounds in change and a book of stamps. They totally ignored the old violin in its case in the corner.

Barry had never thought much of auction houses as he believed that they merely acted as agents in the sale of expensive goods and took a fat commission in the process. His opinion was quickly shattered by Hewitt Jamieson who arrived to discuss the matter of the retrieved violin. He was obviously very knowledgeable and sat opposite Barry and asked him to open the violin case and to look at the violin without showing it to him. He then asked him some pointed detailed questions about the instrument.

"Please look at the back of the violin and tell me if it has eight black horizontal marks across it."

"Yes it does" replied Barry bemused by the question.

"And on the front is there a short scratch next to the bridge?"

"Yes there is!" Barry answered beginning to understand. "I take it that when a valuable instrument goes missing the police inform all you top auction houses to look out for it?"

"Correct" replied the expert. "We have been waiting for this violin to show up for nearly two years so the owner will be very happy that it has turned up! Perhaps you know that it is one of the original violins made by the Stradivari family in Cremona in the north of Italy, in the seventeenth or eighteenth century?"

"Presumably it was insured against theft though?" Barry asked.

"Oh yes. The owner would have been paid out on his claim, but then the violin becomes the possession of the insurance company and they would like to have it back. They then make a deal with the original owner and everyone is happy. Sometimes the original owner doesn't want it back in which case the insurers sell it elsewhere, but in this case I should imagine that the Philharmonic will be very pleased to have it back."

"And is there a reward for finding it?" asked Barry.

"Well that depends on the circumstances. Insurance companies never pay the police for doing their job if an item is recovered simply by a member of the public handing something into them, but in a case like this I do believe that they will be paying something to you for your efforts!"

"Thanks for that" replied Barry with a smile. "I shall then have to work out who any reward belongs to!"

"Well certainly not the thief!" Hewitt replied, clearly an honorable man who did not believe in encouraging theft of any sort. "Just leave it with me and I will let you know the position." He signed for the violin and tucking it under his arm took it away with him.

CHAPTER THREE

A few days later Graham came back to Barry's office with his parents who were very old and fragile, but charming people and just anxious that they were doing the right thing by their lost son. They missed him badly as clearly he had been the bright one in the family and they were sad that he had divorced his wife as they adored his little daughter. There were no bad feelings there, but they believed that the wife had been well paid out by the divorce settlement and she should not benefit financially any further from Stephen's death.

The problem was that they believed that most of Stephen's money should go to his daughter, which meant that it would be managed by her mother which they did not think was a good idea. She was not good with money. Barry explained to them that if they were the Administrators of Stephen's estate then they could control how the money left to the daughter would be spent, but he had to admit that it was bound to finish up in the hands of the child's mother, so they would have to wait and see. First they had to make their application to the Court to be appointed as Administrators of their son's estate when the judge would see the problem and make his own judgment.

The parents were horrified when they heard the story of the violin and were quite different from Graham in their approach and wanted no part of it. They saw at once that they had no right to benefit from the return of the violin as it should have been handed in to the police lost property office by Stephen when he found it, but they felt sad that he had even thought of making a present of it to them. He was a good boy, but perhaps not so honest as he could have been, they said. Graham had other ideas and was wincing quietly sitting next to them and listening to them while he was thinking of the missed opportunity. It was none of his business now, but he felt hurt as he was the one who had found the violin in the attic and felt he should be rewarded.

Barry got on with his work tidying up all the papers and documents to submit to the Court with his application for the parents to be made Administrators of Stephen's estate. Eventually the day of the hearing arrived and they all trooped over to the little court room which had been allocated to them for the private hearing and sat around the table facing the judge.

The District Judge was a wise elderly woman and she had studied all the papers and was clearly in possession of the facts when she asked various members of the family about their relationships with each other. She knew her job was to have the interests of the young child at heart and she did not like the thought of any of the assembled group having their hands on all the money.

"I have considered all the evidence before me and listened to the evidence given by members of the family present and I have decided that the estate of the deceased should be managed by the Official Solicitor."

So it was out of their hands, and Barry felt slightly relieved that he did not have to answer to any members of the family any more about the matter as there was so much bad feeling between them. He spent the next few days sending all the papers relating to Stephen's estate over to the office of the Official Solicitor. They always took a few days to reply to his letters, and much to Barry's annoyance they constantly picked arguments with him in their correspondence about which parts of the estate they were responsible for and which parts were not under their jurisdiction. Barry had thought that they would now look after everything and that he could retire from the picture. That was not to be the case.

Stephen had taken out several life insurance policies in his lifetime which named different Executors in each case. One was in the name of his parents and another in the name of his daughter, so the Official Solicitor's office informed Barry that they would not be looking after the payments due under those policies. They were very particular about following the Court Order to the letter and this did not include managing any finances which were not strictly in the name of the deceased. So Barry was informed that he was very much back in the picture and realised that he had to keep a Trust Account for the parents and for Vicky while she was still under-age, and he informed the parents and Helen, the widow, accordingly. He immediately opened an investment account in the name of the beneficiaries, but after only a few months both parents died and so everything was now left to little Vicky.

The insurance company which had paid out for the lost violin informed him that they had settled the repayment of the claim for the lost violin and they had been asked by the beneficiary to pay a reward to him of five thousand pounds and enclosed a cheque for that amount made payable to him. Barry was in no doubt that this belonged to Vicky and he promptly paid the cheque into his client account and then paid a client account cheque for the same amount into her investment account and informed the family accordingly. Graham was furious and demanded that some (if not all) of the reward money should have been paid to him, especially as he had not benefited from his brother's estate at all. Barry assured him that it had been entirely a matter for Stephen to decide who was to benefit from his estate when he died, but Graham was not happy about that and stayed miserable for the rest of his life. Barry never saw him again.

Vicky's investment account earned her considerable interest over the years, and when she was eighteen her mother wrote to Barry asking him to pay over to her daughter the whole amount which he did. Vicky wrote a "thank you" letter to the solicitor who had looked after her money for so many years but she had never met.

THE END

Broken Promise

CHAPTER ONE

Even through the closed curtains over his bedroom windows Philip could hear the birds singing and the wind blowing through the leafy beech trees. It was still quite early in the morning but he liked to wake up early in the country as it was still all quite new to him. He had been brought up in the suburbs of London but now he was enjoying the totally different style and pace of country living—especially in a lovely old country pub. He jumped out of bed and dressed quickly, putting on his old togs as he was well aware that there was much work for him to do. There had been the usual crowd in the bar the night before, so he went downstairs to start clearing up and wash all the empty glasses and polish the old wooden tables to bring back that lovely sweet clean smell and pleasant atmosphere to the saloon bar which he liked so much. He was enjoying his new life and the feeling that he was doing something useful and making so many new friends.

He switched on the lights as he entered the dark silent bar. The acrid smell of stale cigarette ends and half empty glasses filled his nostrils but he did not mind that as he knew that it would only take him a few moments to clear up the place, and quite automatically he opened all the doors and windows and started to pick up all the empty glasses and put them carefully into the washing machine. Soon it was all done and he was dusting and polishing the furniture.

He had left Gladys sleeping in bed, but he was used to that and happy just to leave her to recover from her normal drunken slumber. It was always the same these days, but that was all part of his agreement with her. He fully intended to keep his part of their deal which was to manage and look after the bar, and in due course he knew she would leave the entire pub to him. She was much older than he was but neither of them minded that. It was more of a business relationship than a love match and neither of them were really very sexy. They had never discussed marriage, but that was out of the question as she was still married to Bill with whom she had never had any children but nevertheless they both continued arguing about their financial settlement. Bill had left her some months ago and agreed that he would keep one of his pubs (as he owned several in the district) and leave her with the "Horse and Groom". That was not enough for Gladys though, and she was argumentative and tough. So she had been to see her lawyer in Beaconsfield to progress the claim she had instructed him to make against Bill for a better maintenance settlement and the lawyer simply followed her instructions and kept arguing. Bill was a wealthy man and had spoilt her during their marriage together, and she was now used to all the finer things in life which she had no intention of giving up just to slave away keeping a pub going on her own.

Philip was the answer to her prayers. He had come into the pub one evening when she was feeling really depressed, and he had started chatting to Gladys about how he was fed up with the London City life and would love to give it all up to come and live in the country. It was his dream. Gladys reacted immediately and made sure that he came back to see her, and when she was sure that he was genuinely interested in her and in the pub life, she made the suggestion to him that he could move in to live with her. Philip took her up on it and was overjoyed at the prospect of a new life in the country. They quickly devised a plan which became a verbal agreement that if he stayed with her and did all the "man's" work in the pub then she promised that she would leave the pub to him in due course. He was much younger than she was, but that was all the better as he was fit and able, and was quite attracted to Gladys and her feminine quirks. She made him laugh and they seemed to hit it off quite well. They couldn't get married because she was still married to Bill, and was likely to stay legally married to him while he kept on arguing with her, but that didn't prevent her from getting on with her life and she was completely open with Philip about this, who totally agreed with her plan and looked forward enthusiastically to this change in his life style.

The Horse and Groom was a popular pub in the district and it had been there tucked away in the Chiltern Hills for many years. Half way between two villages, and off the main road, it really only attracted customers who were prepared to drive there, so there were no problems with local youths or drifters. It was a regular meeting place for local farmers and businessmen, usually at the end of the day before they went home to their wives. Philip fitted in with this ritual very well after his years in the City of London, and many hours were spent discussing the troubles of the world and the local community.

The name of the pub gave away the fact that in years gone by, that part of the country had relied totally on horses for transportation. Even now horses were very popular in the area, especially with the younger members of the community and there were not many families who did not own at least one pony for their children. One of Philip's jobs in the pub was to keep the horse brasses which were nailed to the wall well polished and they always looked splendid on their long leather straps around the fireplace, especially in the winter months when the fire was full of blazing logs.

Most of the customers came in on a Friday evening when they left their wives at home with the children so it was usually a very noisy male gathering. Philip liked that too, as it meant that the conversation could include all the latest bawdy jokes going around. Gladys enjoyed being the only female in the crowd and always called herself "one of the boys". She was good at introducing them all to each other and made sure that her pub continued to be the heart and soul of the village. She always introduced customers to each other and made sure that they knew where to find the local plumber, chimney sweep, or whoever was needed to keep the community self-contained.

Gladys had lost most of her good looks but she had once been quite a "blonde bombshell". She still had that glint in her eye and knew how to chat up the men she fancied. Her figure had filled out a bit but that was only to be expected as she was well into her fifties. Now she just looked miserable most of the time which became one of the regular jokes in the pub—especially against Philip—but he could take it and always had a swift witty response. She did not have any children and her marriage had not been a happy one as she had made it clear to her husband that she was only interested in security and a good style of life—financially. Even her motor car had to be a Rolls Royce with the number plate "GLAD 1".

The local men who congregated in the Horse & Groom were happy to exchange stories over their drinks and to play darts or shove-halfpenny. This game was taken very seriously on a specially polished board which Philip treasured and looked after very well. He kept several sets of halfpennies of different standards which were dished out to players depending on their ability to play the game. He became the judge and jury in deciding who had qualified to be promoted to use the next best set. It was a very simple game and involved placing a halfpenny on the edge of the board and then tapping it with the palm of the hand with just strong enough force to send it sliding up the board so that it stopped between the next two lines marked on the board which were not already occupied by any of the opponent's halfpennies. The fun involved making your halfpenny tap the other player's pieces off the board in the process of making all your six halfpennies come to rest between those lines before he did. The loser would then buy the next round of drinks.

CHAPTER TWO

Steven was new to the village and, like Philip, he had come away from living in the big city to find a better life in the country. He had recently married Alison and they had found a small house on the edge of the village which she loved. Steven went off to work every day in London as a solicitor for a big firm and as the trains were so frequent he was usually back home well before 7pm, so they always enjoyed a good long evening together. There were no children yet but Alison hoped that they would have a family life soon. In the meanwhile she enjoyed the country life and was happy to see that Steven had very quickly found the village pub and was wasting no time in finding new friends there. The joke between them was that they had really wanted to leave London because they found that all their friends there were always trying to entice them into the local pub and seemed to have no other interests at all. This would always go on until closing time by which time most of them were drunk and not at all good company. Neither of them enjoyed this very much—especially at weekends—and decided that there must be a better life in the country. Steven found this to be the case as his new chums in the pub were very different from the regulars in the London pubs he had frequented, and he was soon learning many interesting things in starting his new country life.

When Gladys heard that there was a new solicitor in the pub, she wasted no time in homing in on Steven with her legal problems and soon Philip was inviting him to stay on after closing time to discuss their personal problems—usually concerning Gladys and her divorce proceedings. Alison just got used to the fact that Steven would probably be late home on Friday evenings. She felt happy in the knowledge that the pub was full of men only, so there was no competition as she was a jealous woman at heart.

It was a warm summer Friday evening and Steven arrived home early. He kissed Alison at the front door and they wandered into the garden together.

He loved the view over the Chiltern Hills and he always felt so lucky to have found this little farmhouse. It was all so new to him as he had never had a home in the country before.

"Well I suppose you are off to the pub now?" Alison asked with a smile, just assuming that he would follow his usual procedure on a Friday evening to disappear and leave her alone for most of the evening.

"Yes I think so darling" he replied. "You don't mind do you?"

"No, of course not! You have a good time and don't be too late. Get some eggs while you are there. I am sure Gladys gets them directly from the farmer."

Steven drove off and was soon making his way into the pub which was surprisingly deserted for a Friday. Too early perhaps.

"Hi Steven!" Philip called out casually from behind the bar. His pipe was hanging out of his mouth as usual and he was wearing the same old sports jacket. He continued washing some glasses and then poured out the pint of ale which he knew Steven always liked to drink.

"Busy day?" Philip continued in his affable way.

"Not bad" Steven replied, "Good to be out of it though. How lucky you are to be in the peace and quiet of the country !"

"Not a bit of it! Gladys has been on my back all day." It sounded like a typical moan.

"What's the trouble?" Steven asked as they sauntered out into the garden holding their drinks.

"Oh her husband thing . . . it just goes on, and she likes to take it out on me!"

"Well tell me if I can help at all, but I think she has her own solicitor so there isn't much I can do." replied Steven sympathetically.

"Not really" agreed Philip, "but perhaps you could tell her that she is getting good advice and not to worry so much! The trouble is that she takes it out on me and there certainly isn't anything I can do."

"No, you have to stay out of the way alright or you could make things worse as I am sure that Bill must know about you being here now—and he probably assumes that you are contributing to the housekeeping!"

"Oh I hadn't thought of that! I do hope not though, as I thought I was making life easier for Gladys and not bringing her any more troubles."

Suddenly there was a shout from the kitchen. It was Gladys:-

"Are you going to do nothing all evening?" she screamed. "Get back in here and clear up the bar!" She knew that she could be heard by the few customers who were now gathering in the bar, but she didn't care about that so long as they knew that she was the boss and would not hesitate to tell any of them to leave if they complained.

The evening in the pub was as jolly and noisy as usual and later when it was emptying and the clientele were making their way home, Philip asked Steven to have a drink with him. They were soon joined by Gladys who could be calm and quite pleasant when she wanted to be, and she soon began to confide in Steven and tell him all about her divorce troubles and legal problems. Steven listened attentively and sympathised with her, but assured her that she was probably being well looked after by her solicitor and she should put her trust in him. Nevertheless it was clear that she was angry with the situation and was not a happy woman. The more she went on and on, the more Steven realised that she was being well looked after by her solicitor and there was nothing he could do to help her any further, but just out of good manners he had to stay and listen to her complaints and moans about her position. He felt lucky to be able to get away at last and then when he got home late and found Alison tucked up in bed he found it difficult to explain that he had been held back so late rather against his will to give some legal advice—and that he had not been flirting with some village girl. She always believed him.

CHAPTER THREE

Friday evenings in the Horse & Groom continued and friendships made there became stronger and Steven was soon feeling that he knew everyone who lived in the village and that he was a part of it. Alison joined him sometimes, but usually she was happy to let him go there alone. Steven noticed that the atmosphere between Philip and Gladys seemed to get worse, but the customers assumed that this was all part of the fun of going to the pub and no one took it seriously. Philip had a great sense of humour and he always entertained the customers with his witty responses to the rude commands shouted to him from the kitchen.

"Are you washing those f . . . ing glasses properly?" she screamed from behind the closed door behind the bar. She wanted everyone to know who was boss.

"Yes sweetheart, don't worry!" replied Philip with a smile raising an eyebrow with disdain.

"I know you are being lazy out there just chatting to your chums! Do some f . . . ing work for a change!"

Things were obviously not good between them, but when Steven asked if all was OK, Philip just smiled and told him that Gladys was just going through her menopause like all women, and that no one should take any notice of her outbursts.

Steven was getting quite good at shove-halfpenny after nearly a year of playing the game and he was quietly awarded the privilege of being handed the best set of half-pennies to play with. This put him on equal status with the best of the local farmers and even the boss of the local furniture factory. There was no money involved, but there was definitely a feeling of belonging to the inner clique of friends of the pub and the local community.

Gladys was nearly always drunk by the evening and although Philip liked to manage the bar on his own—and did this very well, there was an atmosphere growing in the pub that all was not well behind the scenes. It became the subject of many bad jokes between the customers, and if ever Gladys did make an appearance it was in a drunken state and she would usually make a scene by arguing with Philip over some trivial matter. He took it all very well but it was becoming apparent that he used his humour cleverly not to embarrass the customers. He was quite prepared to be ridiculed by Gladys if he could prevent a scene which would send the customers away. He was not a stupid man and never lost sight of the fact that the pub was his inheritance and he fully intended to keep his customers happy—and regular.

The scene became much worse when all the customers had gone home because then neither of them had any reason to hold their tongue, and with so much alcohol in both of them the arguments became screaming rows. What Philip did not know was that Gladys was actually very sick and that any doctor would have told her that she should not have been drinking alcohol at all. He thought that she simply became drunk out of habit over the years as he had got used to this, but in fact she was deteriorating quickly and eventually became paralysed and could not move out of her bed.

Philip sent for the doctor who came at once. He saw the problem and told Philip that he was just too late. Gladys died in her sleep that night and in the morning the doctor made the necessary arrangements for the body to be taken away. Philip closed the pub and telephoned personal friends who all gave different kinds of advice. The first thing he had to do was to telephone Gladys' solicitor to establish his legal position. After all, Gladys had promised to leave the pub to him and he had the document which they had both signed to prove this.

CHAPTER FOUR

The solicitor in Beaconsfield was very friendly as he had met Philip in the pub many times. He realised that this was a very serious matter and asked Philip to go and see him. So the next morning Philip tucked the document into his pocket and drove into Beaconsfield feeling secure that the solicitor would effectively change the names on the necessary documents and inform the various suppliers to the pub that he was now the legal owner.

"Do come in Philip" said the solicitor in as friendly a tone as he could muster.

"Please sit down. We were all so sad to hear about Gladys. How are you feeling yourself?"

"Oh, I will get over it" replied Philip, anxious to establish his new position. "I am hoping that you can clear the way for me to carry on the business in my own name now."

Edward Smithson was an experienced solicitor having run his private practice alone in his community for over thirty years and there were very few areas of legal problems that he had not been asked to handle one way or another. Nevertheless he knew that he was going to find this one difficult. He flicked back his silvery hair and slowly sat down behind his large partner's desk to look straight at Philip.

"What makes you think that the pub should pass to you?" he asked quietly.

"Oh that's OK. I have the document with me." Philip replied as he pulled out the agreement which he had tucked inside his jacket pocket and handed it over the desk to the solicitor. Edward took it and opened it. It only consisted of half a page in Philip's clear handwriting showing that Gladys was leaving the pub to Philip on her death. There were the two signatures at the bottom of the page, first that of Gladys and then under her name was Philip's signature and then both names printed clearly under each signature.

There were no other signatures, so apparently there were no witnesses to the document. Edward frowned and put the document down on the desk.

"I am afraid that this will not be sufficient" he said. "Are you sure there are no other documents?"

Philip looked bewildered. "What else do you want?" he asked.

"Well, you must understand that this document is not a Will for several reasons, but principally even though the Court does sometimes grant exceptions with badly written documents, they do always insist that the basic law is complied with, and that for a document to be allowed to be considered as a Will it must be signed by two independent witnesses. There are no witnesses to this document at all, and to make matters worse I have to tell you that Gladys came into this office only about six months ago to make her last Will, and it is quite different from this document!"

Philip was aghast at what he was hearing.

"But she never told me anything about that!" he exploded.

"She must have been out of her mind at the time as we have been living together as man and wife for seven years on the understanding that she would pass the pub on to me on her death!"

"Well I am sorry to hear that" replied the lawyer. "She really should have told you her intentions. As it is, you were never married so you have no rights to any of her Estate, and as an Executor of the Will I must ask you to make arrangements to move out of the house."

"Now just a minute!" retorted Philip deeply hurt and devastated by what he was hearing. "You mean that if Gladys had obtained her final divorce decree from her husband and married me, then things would have been different?"

"Oh yes," the lawyer replied firmly. "A spouse always has a priority interest, subject to those of any children, but a mere partner has no legal right to any possessions or financial claim on the death of his or her partner at all. In fact she could have asked you to leave at any time, but then you could have sued her on the agreement you are showing me now."

"So why can't I sue her Estate now?" Philip asked grasping at straws.

"Because your rights against Gladys under her agreement died with her. It would of course be different if you were a creditor, but as I understand the position she did not borrow any money from you?"

"No" Philip replied lamely. "She just promised to leave me the pub!"

"And then changed her mind as she had every right to do" said the solicitor to close the subject.

"So who is the beneficiary of the pub then? Phillip asked lamely.

"Her sister Bunny has been left everything. There are no other gifts, so apart from her debts and taxes the proceeds of the sale of the pub and all her other assets will go to Bunny".

"But she doesn't want the pub!" insisted Philip. "Can we speak to her and make her see sense?"

"Well I have already informed Bunny of the legal position and after she spoke to her husband they decided that as I was appointed to be the Executor of the Will I should continue to look after their interests. It seems that they do not want to be seen arguing with you or any other old friends of the pub. I suggest that if you want to oppose the Will then you should find a solicitor to represent you. I cannot really help you further."

Phillip was mortified and made his way out of the solicitor's office not knowing where he was going or what he was going to do. He had no money as he always took what he needed from the pub takings. Now he was not even entitled to that. He would just have to think about his position over a few drinks! He was devastated as his entire life and existence had been aimed towards taking over the pub when Gladys died, and now she had committed the ultimate dirty trick against him and had disowned him by completely leaving him out of her Will. They were not married so he had no rights against her estate at all, and to make matters worse, most of the bills and debts created by the pub were in his personal name and he would be liable to pay those—but out of what?

His first step was to contact Bunny whom he knew well and who was respected as a local artist in the village. She was married to Matthew, a property dealer who was not so highly thought of, and many suspected of being involved in many shady deals. Bunny was very upset about the whole thing, but as she did not want to be involved at all she said she was leaving it all to her husband and their solicitor to sort out. Next Philip went to see Matthew who pretended to be sad about Gladys, but then went on to say that he intended to leave all her matters to the lawyers to decide how to handle her estate. It was evident that he could see that there was a lot of money at stake and did not want to lose the opportunity to inherit it through his wife.

Bunny and Matthew lived in a small house in the village where Bunny did her painting, and recently they had invited her elderly mother to stay with them. They also kept two dogs and three cats. It was a very lively household as they also had two young children.

Local gossip travels quickly and a number of old friends and customers went to the pub to find Philip and do what they could to help, but soon he became so depressed that he locked himself into the house and just tried to drink himself to death. Fortunately Harry one of the local regulars had heard the story and when he was driving past the pub early in the evening after Philip had been to see the lawyer, he looked to see if the pub was open. It was firmly shut and there were no lights on in the ground floor, but he saw the light on in the bedroom which he thought was odd so he knocked on the door.

There was no response so Harry shouted up at the window, and when there was no reply he went round to the back door which was fortunately not locked, so he went in and ran straight upstairs where he found Philip unconscious on the floor in his own sick. He immediately telephoned to the police and arranged for an ambulance to come and take him to the local hospital. Philip recovered but it was a near thing for him and had only just been saved by Harry or he would undoubtedly have choked to death.

The news reached Steven several days later, when he noticed that the pub was closed and made some enquiries through some local residents. He contacted the solicitors whom he had been told were dealing with the estate and he was given the shattering news that Bunny, Gladys' sister and heiress of the pub had fallen down the stairs in her own house and had died immediately of her injuries. This meant that unless she had made a Will to the contrary (which it transpired she had not), the pub and all other assets of Gladys would now pass to her husband Matthew. There was much talk and speculation about how Bunny had fallen down the steps in her house which she knew so well, but no details were forthcoming, and the verdict at the inquest later was given as an "accidental death resulting from a fall".

It was only a matter of weeks before Matthew announced that his marriage had not been a happy one and that he intended to marry Jennifer, some local woman who many people in the village seemed to know that he had been seeing.

The wedding was arranged to take place only a few months after the tragedy of Bunny's death and the celebration party was arranged to take place in another of the village pubs. He had his own circle of friends so none of the village locals were invited. During the course of the wedding party, Matthew's house caught fire, but before the fire engine could arrive, it had burned to the ground taking with it his mother-in-law (Bunny's mother) and the domestic animals caught in the blaze. Fortunately the children were at the party so they were saved.

Matthew did not bother to have the house rebuilt as he simply claimed against the insurance company for his loss and went to live in another village nearby.

CHAPTER FIVE

Philip was eventually allowed out of the hospital, but he was a very sick man now and had still not recovered one penny of Gladys estate. He had found a solicitor in Slough to represent him with the benefit of Legal Aid, but the case was getting nowhere, and to make matters worse he heard that the solicitor he had chosen was himself in serious trouble with the Law Society and this was reflected in the poor attention he gave to his cases. The next thing Philip heard about the man was that he had committed suicide by shooting himself with a shotgun in his own office.

He did not know where to turn to, so he telephoned Steven and arranged to visit him in his London office. It was a very sad and sick man who made his way to Steven's office that day. He was broken in body and spirit but determined to rescue something out of Gladys' estate which he felt strongly he had earned and deserved. Steven listened to the full details of the story told by his sick friend and promised to do all he could. It appeared that all matters concerning the estate had been passed by the law firm which had acted for Gladys in Beaconsfield to a small firm of solicitors in the village—Hendersons—who would know all the parties involved and were now acting for Matthew. Steven didn't like that and told the partner dealing with the matter that he would be fighting the estate to make a claim for a substantial payment to be made to Philip.

Steven was in his element now as this was a case which he could put his heart and soul into. He knew about the flaws in the law and how it could be manipulated to arrive at injustice. He fully intended to throw the book at Hendersons and to claim all costs against them and the estate they were representing for keeping Philip out of the money which all Steven's local witnesses would give evidence to show that Philip was the rightful beneficiary of Gladys' estate and that even failing that plea, then he should be kept by the estate for the rest of his days in the manner which he had been promised in the agreement he had made with Gladys who had benefited from his efforts for so long without giving the reward due to him.

Any judge would see the danger in approaching such a case lightly by considering only the financial element. It was already a horrific story with the death of the owner of the pub probably leading to the death of her own sister and her sister's mother. The death of Philip's solicitor was probably not related to the story, but who was to know? It could have been. Where was Matthew at the time? Why did he show no interest in any of the related incidents? He had never appeared again.

Steven knew from personal experience that most small country firms go in fear of being opposed by big firms of London solicitors. There is actually no logical reason for this as all English solicitors are trained in the same way by the same Law School, and pass the same examinations to be admitted as practising solicitors, but nevertheless that fear of heavyweight firms remains and Steven intended to make full use of it. Having an office only a stone's throw from the High Court could have something to do with it, as country law firms need to make use of a London agent to set a case down in the High Court. That increases the costs enormously.

Steven left no doubt in the mind of his opponent that he fully intended to apply to the High Court and would be setting the matter down for a full hearing with an application for all legal costs to be paid by the estate unless an offer was made to pay Philip a just and fair compensation for his loss of the pub. The meagre document which Philip had signed with Gladys may not have entitled him to inherit the property, but it was definitely evidence of her honourable intention. This would then be fully backed up by the evidence of the delay in Gladys' divorce case. There were also many local witnesses just longing to see justice done. Philip had made many friends who would not let him down.

Hendersons soon established that their client's heart was not in the case and it seemed that he was probably not looking forward to any kind of close investigation into his other businesses and family mishaps. So Steven was not surprised when an offer was made by Hendersons to settle the case by agreeing that Philip should be paid a substantial amount and their client would pay all the legal costs incurred. He knew that he was very unpopular in the area and that there would be many witnesses who were available to give evidence in support of Philip's case.

Philip accepted the offer and was pleased to note that Steven's fees had also been fully paid out of the estate. He showed his appreciation by going up to London to take Steven out to lunch, but he was a very sick man by then. He shuffled into Steven's office with the same old pipe hanging out of the corner of his mouth and he was beginning to smile again. Steven did not enjoy explaining to Philip how to claim his state benefits, when they both knew that only months before they had been talking about the improvements he would be making to a lovely country pub and living there proudly at a good standard as its landlord. The Rolls Royce motor car would still have had the number plate "GLAD 1" but that had now been sold.

Philip was now living in his parents' part of the country again down in Kent. They had heard about his disappointment, but like good parents do, they had rallied to help him when they saw how sick he had become. He never recovered fully, but he was well taken care of by them and soon he met a local girl and started a new relationship with her. He was still sick and badly damaged inside though, and he died some six months later penniless and with a broken heart.

THE END

EPILOGUE

Matthew had never been popular in the village as nobody trusted him, so nobody kept up with news about him or his new lifestyle with his new young wife on the coast, but eventually his solicitor let it slip in the pub that he had heard from professsonial colleagues that there had been a terrible accident at sea off the coast of the town where Matthew had gone to live.

It seems that a small boat with two people on board had gone out to sea and were in trouble so one of them had tried to get attention of the lifeboat on shore by firing a Very pistol. The pistol must have been fired accidentally below decks in the vicinity of some spare petrol cans as there was a large explosion and the boat sank with both parties on board who were never found.

The Horse & Groom remained a sad sight on that quiet Buckinghamshire back road for many months as the legal owner never appeared to take any interest in returning there. Eventually it came up for sale in a local property auction sale and was only noticed in the catalogue by accident by one of Steven's legal friends who happened to be there on behalf of a client selling another property.

The property had deteriorated to a shocking state so it was not so surprising that the bidding stopped at such a low figure, but the young lawyer was well aware of its potential so he topped the bid and soon sold it on for double the price to a renowned property developer who turned the site into three lovely homes within a short space of time.

There is absolutely no evidence that there was ever a pub on that site.

Roger the Dodger

CHAPTER ONE

I first met Roger in one of those popular Chelsea wine bars in London. He was very smartly dressed in a very new dark blue suit and clearly an expensive well ironed white shirt with double cuffs and dazzling gold cuff links showing the emblem of some important country club or military regiment. I didn't notice which at the time but I soon discovered that Roger belonged to a number of different prestigious golf clubs, or even if he didn't actually belong to one, it seemed that he would still find a way to visit it whenever he chose to. That was his way. He was quite short in stature but stood out in a crowd, not only because he dressed so immaculately but also because he was a good mixer and conversationalist. I soon discovered that he was also popular because he was generous and usually the first to buy a round of drinks. That was just his way and it made him many friends and business acquaintances. I do not remember him showing off in any way, but somehow he always seemed to be reasonably familiar with any subject which was raised. He seemed to have many friends and I was pleased to be quickly included with those around him who met almost every weekday evening after a day's work before going home or on for dinner somewhere. It was a pleasant ritual and continued in this way for two or three years in either one bar or another.

Most of the crowd were bachelors, or divorced like me, as was Roger, but either way we were always pleased to make the acquaintance of one or other of the pleasant young ladies who also liked to join in the group. It was a good mixed bunch and we all enjoyed each other's company. There was a very pleasant atmosphere in the bar and most of the regulars there soon became good friends and if they had not made previous arrangements for the evening would often go out to dinner together.

I had only recently started a one man private practice as a solicitor having left a large company to go out on my own, and although I was happily working from my own flat I was beginning to think that my practice would definitely run more efficiently from an office with all the usual facilities and a secretary to do my typing. Roger had recently acquired a large office block in Mayfair, he told me, and although he was filling the business suites and offices quite rapidly he said that he would be happy for me take one of the smaller suites in exchange for my occasional legal assistance. This suited me very well and I took him up on his offer. Perhaps I didn't realise it at the time, but Roger was opening the way for me to become a sole practitioner in one of the most prestigous area in the country. This was the area where all the most successful businessmen aspired to have a presence—even if it was only a token office for their activities elsewhere, and they always needed a solicitor sooner or later, if only to assist with the simplest of legal documents and company papers. It was a big step up for me and I was grateful especially as we all got on so well together socially.

I was soon instated into one of the suites in the large sophisticated office block and was pleased to note that it was run by a small clique of friends who all contributed some different input into the organisation. They all had different jobs to do and there was even a man in the basement who turned out fresh sandwiches every day for a very reasonable price. Many of them seemed to have a legal problem of one sort or another so within a very short space of time I was adding to my list of clients without even having to try.

There was only room for one car in the office garage, so naturally as the boss Roger occupied this, and every day would begin with the arrival of his new white Rolls Royce. Hardly a day went by without some new arrival moving into one of the office suites, and it took me a long time to discover that Roger had never actually bought a lease for the premises as he said he was still negotiating terms with the firm of accountants who were looking after the assets of the previous occupiers who had gone into liquidation. It was all very hazy and vague, but nobody discussed the situation as it was none of their business. It was all down to Roger and he seemed to be perfectly happy with everything.

Roger was as good as his word and every time any of his new tenants told him about a legal problem, he would pass them on to me to handle. I had only been in private practice for about two years, but I was learning fast how many different types of problems people could be faced with which they just did not have sufficient knowledge of the system to be able to deal with. So suddenly my scope of work enlarged enormously and I was very pleased with that.

Sven for example, was an interesting Swedish chap who had just arrived from Mexico. He had been working with a food company there, who had discovered a plant growing only in that country which they were calling "Sweetit". He said it was much sweeter than sugar and did not have any of the bad qualities of sugar. It was not harmful to teeth or the digestive system as it did not contain any carbohydrate. It seemed that the problem was to get it recognised and marketed in the UK and other countries in the European Union as there was bound to be strong opposition to it in markets which had been dominated by natural sugar even with all its medical problems. Sven had come to London to work with big boys in the city to set up groups of companies to raise the necessary capital to ensure that the new Sweetit would be a market success.

Sven's new companies were quickly formed to promote the new product, but it could be foreseen that he would meet many difficulties with whole economies such as in Jamaica being threatened by the replacement of sugar on the open market. He had to tread carefully, and of course he had to start by getting his product recognised by the food authorities in each country he intended to market it. He knew that it would take some time to get it off the ground, so he did not flinch from promoting the sale of shares in his company which was quoted on some Stock Exchange and initially valued at about fifty cents each.

Everyone in the block was impressed and busily buying his shares and telling their friends to do likewise, so it was not surprising when Sven showed us all that the value of the shares in his company had risen to eighty cents. News travels. Those closest to him bought more shares than others, but everyone had to participate. Roger made sure of that.

I suppose I was bound to become more involved professionally, as Sven was making deals with new agents in other countries and was appointing them to represent him. They needed contracts authorising them to do so which I was drafting and sending around for approval and signature. It was all very exciting and a novel experience and I was getting well paid by him into the bargain. Perhaps I was the only one to be paid, though, as one day Sven just vanished and it soon became apparent that Sweetit was all just a hoax which Sven had run for as long as he could keep selling his shares and obtaining loans to continue with his fraudulent project. The share price dropped until dealings were suspended. Sven disappeared and was never heard from again.

Roger loved that kind of thing and we had to admit that Sven had fooled all of us even though some were angry about him abusing his friends. His groundwork had been so good and his backup material very thorough with his meetings in the City and with government officials. It was only held against him that he had used his friends and even cheated those who were helping him to achieve his greedy goal. He made no friends that way.

Roger was not like that at all, and when he seized upon a new business venture he wanted to take friends and partners with him to enjoy the fruits of his success. He laughed at Sven and predicted that one day soon someone would catch up with him, but that would not be our concern. Some of Roger's friends did not approve of his methods either, but often it was too late to object. On one occasion for example, Roger invited some forty of us friends and acquaintances to a sophisticated open-air club in the London area for a barbecue garden supper in its exquisite grounds with many waiters and all the trimmings one expected from such an establishment. The combined bands of the Coldstream Guards and Blues and Royals were providing the music as Roger had convinced them that he had been an officer in their regiment. It was then that I recalled that he actually kept a full "Blues and Royals" uniform of that guards regiment behind his office door which was enough to encourage anyone to believe that he had been commissioned into that regiment. He had also fooled the management of the Club into believing that he was one of their members. I subsequently heard that neither of the bills for the band or the catering were paid, but none of his friends knew this until it came to light several months later.

So we knew about Roger, but still enjoyed his company and just made sure that we were not personally involved in any of his schemes or shady deals. Then he went away for a few days and during that time I was surprised one morning to receive a telephone call from him. He was lying on a Florida beach he said, and had overheard an interesting conversation. In a nutshell, he quickly explained while I listened avidly, that he had overheard in a conversation that one of the largest hotel companies in Italy had decided to sell off a huge area of land in the centre of Florence which they had bought some years previously with the intention of developing it into hotels, shops and apartment blocks. They had not yet found a buyer, but they would be holding a meeting in Rome the following week to discuss the marketing strategy of such a large prospective development site. He had somehow convinced the participants that he represented some large development contractors in England who would be interested in such a scheme.

Roger's intuition had gone into full gear as he visualised the marketing potential of such a project, and remembering that I had once worked in Italy and had a knowledge of the language he asked me whether I would care to accompany him to attend the meeting if he could arrange to be invited. His intention was to indicate to the Italian company that he represented a large construction group in England and to take away full details of the planning consent for him to put to one of his big English companies who would be interested in such a project. The commission payable on such a deal would be enormous.

Of course he charmed the Italian executives he had met, who quickly invited him to attend a meeting and we all met in Rome the following week. As good as his word as usual, Roger had booked the two of us into one of the top hotels in the Via Veneto and was ready to pay all the necessary expenses and more. The meeting with the hotel group was extremely civilized as the Italians have always known how to flatter one and be good hosts—especially when they can see some benefit at the end of the tunnel. They gave us all the information which we asked for, and which would be quite sufficient to brief any interested property development company at home who were prepared to come with us and take us on board in one way or another.

On returning to London all the information was passed to David in our social group who ran a very efficient architects' practice, and within a few weeks he had prepared a very plausible set of drawings and plans to present to the Italian authorities. This project could have developed into a very good success story, and probably would have done so in any other European country, but anyone who knows the Italians at work will know that such a story could not end in that successful and happy way. The Florentines more than any other Italians are swamped by local laws and impossible traditions, especially when it comes to the proposed development of any of the age-old historical territories within their precinct. So the plans were passed from one department to another without any definite decision being made and no permissions were given to commence any part of the development. Many different reasons were given for the delays, such as the problem of deciding whether the number of residential properties to be constructed compared well with the number of hotel rooms, or whether there was a sufficient number of shops and offices allowed for. And so it went on and no decision was made. I lost interest in the project eventually, but heard about ten years later that the local planning authority had given permission for an Italian company to undertake the development of the area. No doubt a few shekels found their way into a few pockets along the way!

Roger never worried about his plans going awry as he always seemed to have so many irons in the fire, but as I did like the man it would have been nice to see some of his schemes really hit the jackpot. As it was he relied on the income from his office lettings and the occasional property deal which he became involved in with a few of his chosen friends—who changed from time to time.

One evening he came into the bar with a pleasant American chap who told us that he was going to be involved in one of Roger's property deals in the West End. Damian had been involved in property in one of the southern American states, but jokingly told us that he was happy to get away from some woman who was making his life a misery there. He enjoyed Roger's company and had promised to back him financially in a new deal which all sounded very familiar but as usual we wished them lots of luck, and secretly doubted whether anything would come of it.

It came as no surprise to me when the two of them came into my office and asked me to draw up a partnership agreement, and I was happy to oblige. Then I heard that Roger had asked an insurance broker friend in the building to take out life policies on them both for the benefit of each other in case either of them had some kind of accident before the scheme was completed. That was a common enough procedure and protected them both. It seemed that Damian had his money tied up in some private Swiss Bank in Geneva and they had arranged to travel there together the next day to take it out and bring the cash to London to have it ready to invest in the property they needed for their enterprise.

The next telephone call I received from Roger gave me a terrible shock as I was just not prepared for it. I had been enjoying a relatively peaceful life without having to suffer from any major events to upset anyone, when suddenly there was my major client and good friend telling me that he was telephoning me from his hotel in Geneva to say that Damian was dead. Dead? I couldn't believe my ears! Roger was clearly very upset and went on to explain what had happened so far as he knew. Damian had hired a car to drive from the hotel to his bank in Geneva alone that morning to collect the cash as arranged, and had left Roger in the hotel. Roger said that he had never enquired which private bank Damian used, as this was none of his business, and he had just waved him off after breakfast and expected to see him back in time for lunch with the cash in his pocket.

The police had been informed that a car had been seen crashing into Lake Geneva just outside the town. They had immediately organised for the car to be lifted out of the lake when they found poor Damian's drowned body in the back seat. That seemed strange as he was alone in the car and there was no money in his pocket. Fortunately his hotel key was in his pocket, so the police were able to quickly inform the hotel of the tragedy and make contact with Roger. There was no evidence of any foul play and it seemed that the car had simply driven into the lake at about the only place along the road where there was a gap in the wall and this was possible. The road follows the side of Lake Geneva for a long way and only in one or two places does it dip down to be level with the lake to make it at all possible for a car to swerve into the lake. But why should it have done that? Nobody ever discovered.

Roger was telephoning me to pass on the dreadful news to the staff in his building and to report the matter to anyone whom I considered should be informed. The police had asked him to stay in the hotel while they were making their investigations as this would take a few days, but Roger was clearly very upset about the incident as were all his staff and friends as the news spread like lightning. Everyone had liked Damian, and even though Roger also had his supporters it soon became clear that all his friends and acquaintances were dividing themselves into two distinctly opposite camps. On one side they believed that an unfortunate accident had occurred and that as Roger had been in the hotel he could not have had anything to do with it. On the other side they believed that only Roger knew that Damian was going to collect a large amount of money from his bank and that somehow he had arranged for an ambush or at least someone to take the money from Damian and then ensure that he finished up at the bottom of the lake.

The police took all the statements they could, but could not find any reason to detain Roger so they let him go back to London. There was no trace of any of the money, and as no one knew which bank he had gone to it was not possible to check even whether he had collected the money he said he was going to collect.

Roger was treated with sympathy on his return, but in view of his colourful reputation the gossip soon spread that he must have had something to do with it. He certainly did not behave as though he had suddenly come into a fortune, but then (as his opponents were fond of saying) "He wouldn't would he?" In fact he claimed that he had suffered severely financially from the incident as he had paid for both the airfares and hotel accommodation in Geneva and was asking me to make a claim against the life insurance policies which they had taken out before their trip.

The conversation in the bar began to revolve around the tragic incident and the sad loss of Damian as everyone had liked him and considered him to be a good partner for Roger, but very soon it became apparent that there were those who seriously believed that Roger was directly responsible for the man's death one way or another, and then there was the other group who believed that a man should be considered to be innocent until he was proved to be guilty. The arguments went on for days, and the participants became more entrenched in their views until friendships were broken and some people stopped going to the bar at all for fear of becoming embroiled in another argument over the tragic affair which would not just go away.

I tried to keep my opinions to myself, but as everyone knew that I had been instructed by Roger to look after his legal interests, it was quite obvious on which side of the line I was to be found, even though I kept my feelings to myself unless I was asked any factual questions about the matter. The huge embarrassment for me was to come a little later when I innocently filed the claim with the life insurance company for them to pay up on the life policy and they made their usual personal checks and soon established that in fact Roger was a certified bankrupt and had been for some months. That was something rather important which he had not told me, and of course it meant that he could not be paid anything at all by the insurance company. All payments due to a certified bankrupt are made to the Official Receiver. The bankrupt gets nothing.

When this came to light, the news spread fast, and those who had never liked Roger and clearly belonged to the group who had always believed in his guilt, tried to make matters worse for him by making statements to the police about his previous activities. Many of us had laughed at Roger's activities and personal antics pretending that he had been a Guards officer and also that he had studied for the Bar. It did no harm, and in fact most of us were riding on the back of his false character by taking advantage of his kind hospitality and generosity, but others thought differently and were out to get him. They succeeded as they convinced the police that they should add to their main charge of fraudulently attempting to claim monies from the life insurance company, the lesser charges of improperly posing as a barrister and also as a retired army officer. Under the law, these would only be constituted as offences if he had attempted to gain some unfair financial advantage by so doing, and perhaps he had.

I attended the long trial and although the jury found Roger not guilty of the main charge they did return a guilty verdict on the lesser charges. What surprised me was that the judge sentenced Roger to twelve months imprisonment which I considered to be outrageous for those lesser offences, and was probably only given because the judge thought that he was also guilty of the other main charge in spite of the jury's verdict. We will never know.

I visited Roger in jail, and as expected he was his cheery old self and was probably running some kind of shop for other prisoners as he was so adaptable. His positive attitude and cheerful personality enabled him to get around most people, so I was not really surprised when he suggested that my visit should take place on a sunny afternoon on the seafront of Bognor Regis. This was apparently an easy bicycle ride for him from the prison, and he arrived on time wearing a clean singlet and white shorts and carrying a cool bottle of champagne in the basket of his bike which we devoured on the beach. Oh yes, I had to admire the spirit in the man and I only hoped that he had nothing to do with his partner's demise in Switzerland.

When he came out of jail, Roger went to live in Ireland as a recluse as he could not face all those old mates in London who thought he was a murderer. He came to London some months later and invited me out to lunch which I was pleased to accept as I always enjoyed his company. I was only slightly concerned that he arrived at the restaurant in a brand new Rolls Royce motor car.

Legal Pressure

CHAPTER ONE

The events in this story took place many years ago and I often wonder whether with the changing attitudes in our Society the results would or should be the same today and I must leave the reader to be his or her own judge of that.

The facts were put into motion when Jeremy gave up his first job in civilian life to help his mother with her small property business which was mainly concerned with letting out bedsitting rooms in a few houses in the West End of London. He had been very well brought up in boarding schools and then the army so he was very disciplined and well organised, so it was a simple matter for him to make use of this experience to check on all the rent payments being made by the tenants in the many bed-sitting rooms and to keep a record of these and also to see that the caretakers were doing their job in keeping the properties clean and tidy. They were all a little afraid of him so they did their job well to satisfy him and his standards. As time went by the routine became quite monotonous and boring for him and was taking up less of his time so he decided that he should do something else and start to study for a professional career like most of his friends were doing. He picked on the legal profession as he knew that he was financially stable with the property business behind him, and that he would not have to worry about finances for the five years it would take him to qualify.

Jeremy's mother Marisa was a good looking Spanish woman who still attracted second looks as she walked down the street. She was petite and slim in build and was proud of her long silky hair which flowed over her pretty face drawing attention to her large beautiful brown eyes. The West End of London had been her new home since her husband had deserted her after the war and left her with two children who were at boarding school most of those earlier times. Then Belinda had left school and now lived with friends sharing a flat in Hampstead. Jeremy had just come back from his national service and after trying a few jobs had agreed to help out with her business which she found to be rather strenuous as she was not used to dealing with tenants' problems and company accounts. He was soon running the business on his own and Marisa was happy to be able to travel much more, and particularly to go and visit her family in Madrid. She was happy to see that Julian had decided to study law and she promised that her business would back him financially until he had qualified, as he had made her promise that she would take back the business when the time came.

The time had now come as Jeremy had passed his final examinations and he was just starting his first job with an international finance company in the West End. It all sounded very exciting as he was often travelling to Geneva where his Company had its head office, and other places where they sent him to assist with their legal problems. Marisa saw him on a regular basis when she was in London, but that was less and less as she was now leaving the administration of her business to the caretakers in each of her houses and when she was not abroad she liked to be in the country where she had another property. Jeremy was not happy about this as he didn't trust the caretakers to be honest with Marisa and he was sure that they were cheating her on a regular basis. Renting out furnished rooms was strictly a cash business, and some of the lets were so short that there was not even a proper record being kept of who was where and for how long, but it was no longer Jeremy's business, so he could only warn his mother to be careful and leave her to take whatever steps she considered to be necessary.

Marisa had recently married Henry who was a successful businessman but as he was also too busy to attend to Marisa's property business this was left almost entirely in the hands of her various caretakers. It all seemed to be going well though, and Marisa was very happy with her new life, so she gave little thought or time to her properties which were providing sufficient income to keep her satisfied. She was happily enjoying her new married life and did not want to be bothered with checking the caretakers' accounts. Also she did not want to let them feel that they were not trusted even if the cost of that was to lose some of the income which was properly due to her. Henry travelled a lot in his business and he liked to take Marisa with him and often they were out of the country for several weeks at a time.

It all seemed to run very smoothly, but then one day when Marisa was away and had been abroad for some weeks, the telephone rang in Jeremy's flat soon after he had returned home from his office.

"I am sorry to bother you," the caller began very politely, "but could you please tell me how to reach Mrs Edwards who I believe is the leaseholder of 25 Regents Park Mews."

"Yes," replied Jeremy, "I am her son, but I regret to say that my mother is abroad at the moment so can I help you?"

"Well perhaps you can," continued the caller, "My name is Jason Clarke and I am calling from Cluttons as we are the agents for the Church Commissioners who are the freeholders of Regents Park Mews. We understand that there is a prostitute in your mother's house who is being a nuisance in the Mews by having frequent late night callers who disturb the neighbours. If she does not leave the premises we will have to take proceedings against your mother, so do you think you can help?"

"Oh yes," Jeremy replied airily. "Please leave it to me and I will see that she leaves very soon."

Jeremy immediately called the caretaker at the property and soon realised from the conversation that Giuseppe knew all about the girl. He promised that he would ask her to leave immediately. Jeremy had never really trusted Giuseppe whom he believed to be a shifty character who would not hesitate to cheat anyone—even Jeremy's mother who was employing him—and he was sure that he was stupid enough to bite the hand who was feeding him. So now he didn't believe him, but he didn't really know why. He just felt that there was something wrong, so he decided to check on the position himself.

The next day as he was driving back home from his office he made a slight detour to visit Regents Park Mews. There were four bells on the front door, one for each flat in the building. He decided to deal with the matter himself before speaking to Giuseppe, so he looked for the bell of the flat being occupied by the trouble-maker. That was no problem as she had put a crude paper label by her bell saying "MAVIS". That was enough to make it clear who and what she was. Jeremy rang the bell and was admitted, and as soon as he was in the flat he went into the attack.

"My name is Jeremy Edwards and I am the son of Mrs Edwards who owns this house," he began. "I understand that you are running a business from here and that has to stop!"

"Well I don't know anything about your mother dear" replied the girl immediately on the defensive.

"I was let this flat by Giuseppe and I paid him the rent so I'm staying put!" She looked him straight in the eye and as she was so used to doing with men, she summed him up very quickly. He was looking her up and down and once he had got over the embarrassing introduction and the purpose of his visit, he found himself automatically wondering just how sexy she was.

"I paid him fifty pounds for a month in advance, and he said it was OK for me to stay," she insisted as she started to sit down and cross her legs in front of Jeremy. She was wearing high heeled shoes and showing a lot of her legs which Jeremy couldn't help noticing—and she noticed that he was noticing. He was going to be putty in her hands, she was thinking.

"Fifty pounds!" Jeremy exclaimed "That is much less than the rent you should pay for this flat! I suppose you slept with him as well? OK! Ok! Don't tell me! Look here, the landlords are making a fuss about you being here, so you will have to go anyway!"

"Where to?" she replied miserably. "I will have to find a place, so give me some time!"

"Well OK. But I want you out of here by next week. Is that clear? And just to be sure that you go, I want you to pay me the balance of the proper rent for this flat. I calculate that as being another fifteen pounds per week. Is that OK?"

She seemed to agree without saying anything as she was looking at him in a cheeky way now that she could see that she wasn't being thrown out into the street, and she started to run her leg gently up against his. She winked at him when he didn't take his leg away.

"You don't look as though you need that fifteen pounds, and I'm sure your mother wouldn't know anything about it either would she?" she said putting her hand was on his knee, and Jeremy was quickly beginning to see things her way. As a lawyer, he knew very well that he could not just throw her out into the street anyway, so the deal he had made should be the best way to make her go, and now he could turn his attention to other things.

"What's your real name?" he asked her in a softer tone warming to her touch. She knew exactly what she was doing and he wasn't objecting.

"I'm Jackie really," she said with a saucy smile as she took off her blouse and quickly kicked off her short skirt. She was in charge now and she felt she could eat this boy alive, but she would give him a good time and get him on her side. She was short and slim and although she was not very pretty she had that animal sensuality which was very appealing to a young boy in his prime. Jeremy was not one who would miss out on a golden opportunity like this.

They moved to the bedroom where the sex was short and pleasant for them both and soon Jeremy was dressed again and on his way. He was determined that this was now a matter which was entirely between him and

Jackie and that she would be out of the flat by the following week. She had said so. He had no intention of discussing the matter with Guiseppe as he had clearly been cheating his mother and turning the house into a brothel into the bargain. He would just be sure to tell him very firmly when Jackie had gone that he should not repeat the mistake as they did not want any further trouble with the freeholders.

As a newly qualified solicitor, Jeremy took the law very seriously and he considered his position with Jackie carefully. Under the law he was entitled as a bona fide representative of his mother to serve a formal Notice to Quit upon the tenant, but this would need at least twenty eight days to expire, so he believed that he had found a better solution, by simply obtaining her agreement to leave the flat. No formal Notice would necessary and soon the whole matter would be cleared up and she would be gone.

Jeremy was very disciplined in some ways, and so at exactly the same time on the same day of the following week he was at the house again ringing the door bell, but he was feeling slightly disappointed that the name tag was still there. As soon as he was inside the flat he immediately told her off.

"You said you would be out of here by now!" he exclaimed. "And you haven't even taken your name off the front door!"

"Well I couldn't find a place!" she replied woefully. She was a good actress and she was behaving towards him as though they were old friends.

"Would you like a drink?" she asked cheekily.

Jeremy was furious as he could see that his plan was going wrong already. His legal mind began working and he was wondering whether he should now serve her with a formal Notice to Quit, but if he did that it would have to state clearly that she had a further four weeks to stay in the flat and he didn't want that.

"Look, you promised to go within a week and I don't believe that you have done anything about it!"

"I have been looking—honest!" she replied, almost making him believe her.

"Well you just give me another fifteen pounds now and make it the last one—I don't want you to be here next week—OK?"

"Same deal as last week then?" she replied sheepishly looking up at him in a very sexy way.

"Well OK, but for the last time!" he replied, not feeling at all comfortable, but not knowing how to say no to an open offer of a good fuck. He was a sexy boy and she knew how to turn him on. He had lost and knew it.

Jeremy left the flat feeling very depressed as he realised that he was not getting his way at all, and that there was now a distinct possibility that she would just stay on thinking that she could play with him for as long as she liked. He was not going to let this happen, so he made a firm decision that if she tried the same tactics the following week he would definitely serve her with a legal Notice to Quit. That would see the end of her, even though he would have to wait for four weeks for the Notice to expire.

Another reason Jeremy did not want to use the correct method of serving a formal legal Notice was that he knew that even when the Notice expired after four weeks, a landlord still had to apply to the County Court for an Eviction Order before Bailiffs could be instructed to take action—and then they took another four or five weeks to leap into action to actually remove the Tenant. Then of course there were fees payable at each step of the way—and always there was the big possibility that any of the steps could fail or be returned by the Court if there were any typing errors or other mistakes—a huge possibility with a defendant whose name was in doubt and who had no permanent address. Jeremy had learned from bitter experience of five years as an articled clerk in a solicitors' office that some delays were almost guaranteed in any court process. He was now in a very difficult position especially as he was well aware of the fact that he had never actually taken a case like this himself. He had merely studied the law and knew what he could and could not do, so if any legal action was required he would have to consult another solicitor. He hoped that would not be necessary as he could not see that he would ever be able to retrieve any of the costs from such a defendant. She would just disappear.

CHAPTER TWO

The following week Jeremy was not feeling at all good or positive about his position with Jackie as he drove into the mews. He felt that he had created this situation, but that somehow he had been dragged into it as there did not seem to be any other way of resolving it. His fears were confirmed when he saw that the scruffy name tag still on the door. He rang the bell and waited for what seemed to be a long time before Jackie replied to let him in.

As soon as Jeremy was in the flat he went on the attack and demanded that Jackie should leave. She had clearly not found any alternative accommodation so he told her that he would be serving her with a formal Notice to Quit, but that while she was in the flat she should continue to pay him the fifteen pounds per week. He wanted the full rent paid and if he could have thought of any other legal means to encourage her to leave he would have said so, but he couldn't.

Her response was very strange and distant as she replied to him from the other side of the room—as though she wanted someone else to hear the conversation through the window. Jeremy was perplexed but not unduly concerned, as he was only here to make a last attempt to obtain her promise to move out within the next few days. His demand for her to pay the balance of the usual rent for the flat was in order and he hoped was also acting as a lever to make her want to move on, but it seemed to have a curious effect on the conversation, because she suddenly asked,

"What happens if I don't pay you the fifteen pounds?"

He was nonplussed but replied "Well you would have to move out at once for non payment of rent. But it doesn't make much difference as we agreed that you should move out anyway! So are you going to move out or not?"

"So you say you would put me out?" she persisted pointedly. She was definitely acting strangely and he didn't like it.

"Yes definitely," he replied, with a sinking feeling that he was being forced into the position of having to start a long eviction procedure.

There was a long pause and then suddenly there was noise coming from the bedroom. Two men had been hiding in the double wardrobe there, and they suddenly appeared in the doorway brushing down their plain civilian grey striped suits and straightening their ties. After the first shock of the disturbance Jeremy wondered whether he was being attacked by villains working with Jackie, but this was soon put out of his mind. They were behaving correctly and stood together on the opposite side of the room close to Jackie who now remained silent.

"We are police officers," said one of them, slightly older than the other one. "And we heard all that you said to this young lady and believe that you were demanding money with menaces"

"I was not!" replied Jeremy just about recovering from the shock of their appearance and still very red in the face.

"We heard you say quite clearly that you would put her out if she did not pay you some money! How do you explain that?" he continued.

"That was for the rent she had not paid, and I am going to take steps to put her out anyway as she is acting unlawfully as a prostitute here." Jeremy insisted. Then having almost recovered himself fully he continued to explain to the officers:-

"Look, can't you see? She is turning this flat into a brothel and I have promised the landlords that I would see that she moved out. The small amount she was paying me was only to make up for the rent which had underpaid to the caretaker!"

"Well you are not her landlord, and we believe that you were demanding money you were not entitled to," replied the officer. "As I understand the position she had already paid her rent to the caretakers who represent the landlord, so who are you?"

"The owner of this house is Mrs Edwards who is my mother and she happens to be abroad at the moment so I am looking after her interests."

"She has caretakers to do that, and they let this flat to Jackie, so how come you can just jump in and take their place?"

"Well firstly they should not have let the flat to a prostitute and secondly they did not charge her a full rent. You would think that in the circumstances they would have charged her more—not less! I think you can draw your own conclusions."

"Well it doesn't sound right to me so you will have to come with us down to the station and we can iron all this out down there."

Jeremy was completely shocked, but he truly believed that as a respectable lawyer he should co-operate with the police and went with them quietly, asking one of them to drive his car to the station so that he would be in a position to drive home later. He did not believe that he would be in any trouble as soon as the police officers had fully understood the details of the complicated story. He was wrong. The more they questioned him at the police station, the more they seemed convinced that he did not have the right to ask for that extra fifteen pounds and that he was therefore making unwarranted demands for payment. Jeremy could hardly take the matter seriously, as fifteen pounds was such a small amount to him, but he could see that the officers were adamant in making it the centre of an offence which they were convinced he had committed.

He did not even think of telephoning any of his legal colleagues to come and back him up, as he knew he was entitled to do while in police custody, as he thought that all would be well after the whole matter had been properly explained. After further repetitive questions and answers, he was put into a police cell to read his newspaper while the officers checked with the Crown Prosecution Service whether he was to be charged. He felt confident that he would be let out soon with some kind of reprimand, but on the other hand he did feel slightly uncomfortable with the thought that the officers had more readily believed the story they had been told by the girl rather than his story and explanation for his behaviour. Why had they not summed up the general situation and realised that the girl would have to move out of the flat sooner or later anyway?

Jeremy was feeling very uncomfortable sitting alone in that miserable little cell knowing that somewhere out there in the offices of the Crown Prosecution Service someone totally unknown to him was discussing with those two police officers whether or not to charge him with a very serious offence. Surely they must take into account that his intentions were to get the girl out of the flat and not that he was trying to make a "quick buck". Or would they? They were used to dealing with criminal minds and were probably very suspicious of his motives. The girl would have seen to that when she sent for them and discussed the matter behind his back. Surely they would have the intelligence to realise that he had no need to cheat anyone for fifteen pounds? They only had to assess his style of life to understand that. He should then be warned to keep clear of such dangerous territory, but not charge him and ruin his entire career. Jeremy could not believe that they would be so cruel.

It seemed to be ages before anyone came back for him, but eventually he was let out of the cell and taken to the duty sergeant who told him that he was being charged with the offence of demanding money with menaces. Jeremy was staggered. There was nothing he could say to the very polite police sergeant as he was clearly not the one who had told the story to the Crown Prosecution Service. It was those other two. Was there some kind of alliance between them and the girl? The younger one seemed to be very friendly with her in the flat, and Jeremy had felt that they knew each other quite well. Did they have some kind of pact for free sex? Jeremy wondered about that for a long time as otherwise why would two police officers waste so much time over such a trivial matter?

Jeremy knew that he was now in a very serious position and he was angry with the Crown Prosecution Service for not having taken account of the fact that even if he was unwittingly guilty of some minor offence, he could not possibly plead guilty to having committed it, as he was in a different position from their usual suspects as in his case there was the greater danger that if he was found guilty the Law Society would definitely strike him off the roll of solicitors for having committed a criminal offence—however trivial that may seem to be. He was angry, as he knew that if he wanted to be completely exonerated he would have to take the case out of the hands of the local Magistrates Court (who were renowned for always accepting police evidence) and have it heard in the High Court where he understood that there was a greater chance of being found not guilty by a jury. So he must be sure to be represented there when the time came by a top counsel. He would have to prepare the case well and have it dismissed completely if he was going to stay on the roll of solicitors which had taken him five years to train for. He was not going to throw all that away on the whim of some little tart. He had to smile sardonically at the thought that with her limited intelligence she could not possibly have imagined the amount of trouble she had caused. It was too much to hope that she would be made aware of it and agree not to give her evidence in court.

Jeremy duly appeared in the Magistrates Court the following morning, and when he was asked to plead to the charges which were read out, he simply replied "Not Guilty."

He went back to work the next day and was met by the Chief solicitor who was holding the local paper in his hand. A small article had summed up his charge without printing any of the details.

"What is this all about Jeremy?" he asked in as friendly a tone as he could.

"Oh absolute nonsense!" Jeremy replied, fully prepared to tell the whole story, but he was stopped in his tracks.

"Yes OK," replied his boss, "but I will have to let you go until it is all sorted out. I hope you understand that the Company has enough problems already, so I will arrange for you to be paid for two months, and then we shall have to wait and see how your case goes. I can only wish you the best of luck—and please keep me informed."

He was a good man and sympathised with Jeremy but he had to put the company first.

Suddenly Jeremy found himself at home again without a job and no idea of where to turn to. He knew that it would be months before the case would come up for hearing, so at least he could start to prepare his defence. He knew several young solicitors in the area, so he began to ring around for advice. It was all very well that he had qualified as a solicitor and was now fully empowered to advise others with regard to their legal problems, but it was quite a different matter to actually be there in the limelight himself. Anyway he firmly believed in the maxim "Any solicitor who acts for himself has for a client a fool" and he had to admit that he knew absolutely nothing about the working of criminal cases.

David was a sole practitioner with a small office just behind Harrods in the Brompton Road, and he suggested that they meet for lunch to discuss the whole thing. David had qualified as a solicitor a few years before Jeremy so he had that extra bit of experience which enabled him to advise Jeremy to take his case to a top solicitor who specialised in criminal matters. He knew that Lord Napier had a big well established firm in Lincoln's Inn and who was famous for taking on many big cases which were often in the newspapers. So Jeremy immediately contacted the firm and made an appointment to see the famous solicitor. In the meanwhile David agreed that Jeremy could work as his assistant in the office for a fair salary which suited them both very well.

Jeremy went to see Lord Napier the next day, but when he arrived and was introduced to him he was disappointed to be met with quite a cold response and absolutely no sympathy. He told the full story of the arrest and what led up to it, but Napier was very suspicious and clearly thought there was more to it. He attacked Jeremy by asking why a newly qualified solicitor would put himself in the position of being arrested for demanding a rent of fifteen pounds from a common prostitute? There must be more to it. He said he would wait to see the papers from the Crown Prosecution Service.

In the meanwhile he introduced Jeremy to Larry who was one of his assistants whom he had appointed to take on the case. Jeremy was shocked at being fobbed off in that way as he considered that his case was of vital importance for him to be able to continue with his career. He felt strongly that his case should have taken precedence over the kind of cases which Napier was known for defending such as pop musicians in the headlines who had been arrested for possessing drugs in some fashionable night club. Of course there was more money there in legal costs—and press coverage. He was known to be ambitious and as Vice-President of the Law Society he would become President next year and automatically receive a peerage. Jeremy's case would not have seemed to him to be one to catch the headlines. So even though Jeremy was angry at being passed on to Larry, he went in to see him and to give him the full facts of his case. It could be that Larry would only be responsible for opening the file and making notes of the facts of the case and Jeremy's background. Then he hoped that it would be passed on to a senior Counsel to take into court. He was assured that was going to happen, but in the meanwhile Larry was asking him to go in to see him so many times for him to take so many notes that Jeremy was suspicious that his case was being built up into one which was far away from the truth of the matter.

Jeremy had telephoned his mother in Madrid the day after his arrest to tell her the story of the prostitute and how he had tried to evict her when the agents had telephoned him. He had also told her how he had discovered that Giuseppe had undercharged Jackie for the rent and Marisa immediately agreed that he was probably up to no good as he had not even reported to her that Jackie had moved into the flat. That was in the past now, though, she said, and now it was more important that she should write a letter to Jeremy to confirm that he had full authority to represent her in managing the mews house and to take rent from the tenants. That should put a stop to it all, she said.

Jeremy received the letter after a few days and took it into Larry who did not seem to be at all impressed by this confirmation of Jeremy's position. This surprised Jeremy who had felt sure that it would bring an end to the case, but he was slowly beginning to learn that regardless of his authority he was being accused of committing the criminal offence of making a demand with menaces. Larry tried to convince him that he was in grave danger of being found guilty as he had admitted that he had made the demand for fifteen pounds on each visit, whether he had the authority to do so or not. So it seemed that his defence would rest upon the point of whether he had made the demand "with menaces". Did that include telling Jackie that she had to leave the flat? It seemed so, even though he was asking her to leave anyway.

During those weeks of preparation for the trial, Jeremy was feeling satisfied that any jury would acquit him as soon as they realised that he believed that what he was doing was right—or at least the only way out of a difficult situation. He had learned at Law School that every crime had to contain a "Mens Rea"—the Latin expression still being used in English criminal law books to describe the mental attitude of every criminal who knew that he was doing something wrong. OK, so his story was complicated by the fact that he was not actually the legal landlord, but any sensible person should easily be convinced by any good barrister that he was acting in the best interests of his mother who had provided a letter to confirm that. There was no "mens rea" in this case so he should be acquitted. That was how he thought, and he knew that he had to remain positive, but Larry was not giving him any assurances that the trial would go that way.

After a few weeks he was introduced to Jonathan Davis QC who had been appointed to take his case at the hearing. It was a very short conference during which the QC asked him pointedly whether he would like to plead guilty. Jeremy was surprised that even his own QC had not grasped the point that he had only come all this way in the legal process to be found "not guilty". Any other finding would result in him being struck off the roll and thus losing a whole career he had worked so hard for. He could only make the point again very strongly that the case should never have been brought and that he was innocent of any criminal offence. Davis listened to him and prepared his case for the hearing. That was what he was being paid to do, so he would do it, but for the first time Jeremy felt ominous that his own Counsel had started off their association with such a question.

CHAPTER THREE

Four months went by before the case came up for hearing at the Old Bailey and Jeremy was horrified to see that it was listed to be heard in Court Number One which was the Court where so many infamous murder trials had taken place in the past. Nobody had pestered him with any formalities prior to the hearing and so he just turned up on the day at the appointed time and found Jonathan Davis all dressed up in his barrister's wig and gown with Larry waiting for him in the Court. He surrendered his bail to the police officer in charge of the Court and was then taken down to one of the large cells in the basement under the Court to wait to be called.

The atmosphere down there felt damp and musty. There were many cold shiny bricks and the plastered walls were covered with griffiti and the scrubbed stone floors were well worn. He was offered a cup of dreadful sweet tea which did nothing to take away the feeling of being in the wrong place and wondering how all this had come about. The graffiti on the walls had apparently been made by previous accused prisoners waiting to be tried in the Courts above, and he wondered whether any of the famous prisoners he had read about in his legal studies had sat on the same bench he was now sitting on. There was an eerie silence broken only by the occasional banging of an iron door somewhere down the long corridor or the heavy footsteps of one of the prison officers who had charge of the cells, and one of whom would occasionally just look in on Jeremy and ask if he was OK. They were a pleasant lot and had their duties to perform looking after the prisoners.

Eventually one of the prison officers came to take him upstairs, and to his surprise the steps led directly into the prisoners' box in the middle of the Court. That in itself was a frightening experience for someone like Jeremy and he felt as though he was going on stage for the first time and finding that the curtain had already been raised. The judge was in his place up on the bench in his full regalia and the barristers and instructing solicitors were sitting below him. The Court was packed as was the visitors' gallery above his head. The clerk read out the charges to Jeremy and asked him to plead to each of the charges accusing him of demanding those sums of fifteen pounds "with menaces".

"Not guilty!" he replied firmly and the clerk then said that he should sit down.

The Court process was very thorough and took time, and left Jeremy wondering why they bothered with some of the procedures when it was clear to everyone that the police officers had not conformed with the original arresting formalities properly by not warning him that he had no need to say anything at the time, but the judge said he would overlook that and wanted to proceed with the trial and started swearing in the members of the jury. This again took a considerable time, and although Jeremy knew that he should have not accepted some of the candidates for the jury simply because of their dark looks at him, he wanted to appear to be a gentleman not wanting to make a fuss, so he said nothing and just let the process take its course. He was nursing the persistent feeling that he would not be found guilty as soon as the jury had been convinced that he had not intended to take any money improperly. That should not be difficult for his Counsel, he thought, as they were only talking about fifteen pounds and he had a good full time job with good prospects and no money difficulties. So what was all the fuss about?

The QC representing the Crown led the case for the prosecution was a well seasoned barrister who relished the opportunity to make fun of Jeremy for taking the opportunity of having sex with the girl, and he launched a vicious attack by intimating that he had also taken advantage of his mother's absence abroad to visit Jackie in the flat to demand the payment of money. Marisa was sitting in Court but she was not given the opportunity to tell her part of the story as the barrister thought it was not really relevant to the charges being brought which the prosecuting barrister had made a meal of. It was a lovely case for him. Jeremy felt differently, but he had passed the case to lawyers whom he believed to be experts and soon learned that once it was in their hands it was entirely under their control and he had no say in how it was handled.

Jeremy was called to give evidence in his own defence, and having had no experience of criminal courts or criminal matters he fell into all the traps laid for him by the prosecuting QC and even admitted to having behaved like a fool. It was all over and he was unwittingly signing his own death warrant so it came as no surprise to the gallery when the jury returned after only two hours of deliberation to pronounce that they found him guilty as charged.

The judge was very experienced in criminal matters and he knew that the charges were miniscule compared with most of the matters he usually had to deal with, but nevertheless he had a job to do which would be widely reported, so he pronounced a sentence of six months imprisonment for each of the offences to run concurrently (together) so Jeremy was sentenced to serve six months in prison. Larry soon informed him that he would only have to serve half of this term in an open prison, but Jeremy was still smarting at the finding of the Court and immediately thought about appealing against it. Larry advised him strongly against that for practical reasons, as such an appeal would take at least three months to prepare by which time he could be a free man again. Nevertheless Jeremy was angry as he felt that he had been bulldozed into prison by those two police officers. He would never be able to prove anything against them.

The newspapers loved the story of a solicitor being found guilty of taking advantage of a prostitute and they all made a meal of it as though Jeremy had been running a sex business, but anyway the publicity did him no further harm as the damage had already been done and, if anything, it enhanced his position with his new cell mates. Jeremy was a good mixer and had no difficulty in getting on with them, most of whom had their own interesting stories to tell. Then after a few days he was moved to an open prison in the southern counties and was able to relax for the first time that he could remember. He only had to deal with the problem of the fact that he was now going to be struck off the roll of solicitors.

Those few months in prison were invaluable, as not only did Jeremy meet several interesting people inside prison, but he also joined a few classes and started to take an interest in painting and woodcarving. He would never have done so before. He was treated like a gentleman, and had the respect not only of other prisoners, but also of the prison officers who always liked to have a chat with the inmates to make their own lives easier. They made sure that he was included in all the various sporting activities which included swimming in the local pool and athletics which was organised within the grounds.

The weather was glorious that summer, and Jeremy had never in his life spent such long periods of time lazing on green grass lawns talking to a complete mixture of young men, most of whom had interesting stories to tell—not always happy ones, but usually colourful and often amusing. The accommodation he shared with two other inmates was much better than he had experienced at school and nearly as good as many officers' quarters he had been allocated to in the army. The discipline was very easy, and he was not the first to remark that if a boy had been to an English boarding school he would not have any problems inside an open prison. What he liked most of all though, was the fact that he could help so many people with their real problems, as it was quite beyond the means of most of those he met to even know how to instruct a solicitor for legal assistance, even though this was usually paid for by the state.

There were many curious systems inside the prison which had been devised over the years to bring order to the running of the prison, and one of these was the requirement to apply to the assistant governor in person to ask for anything at all beyond the daily routine. In fact Jeremy found the ordinary routine to be very efficient and the meals to be quite adequate so he had no particular complaints to make, but he did feel that the library could be improved by having a gramaphone/record player made available to allow inmates to listen to classical or other music of their choice and also to be able to play language learning discs if they wanted to study one. So he applied for this and was pleased to see that a record player was in fact provided just before he moved on.

Jeremy left prison after those few weeks with a stronger feeling of freedom than was enjoyed by most of those inmates who would soon find their way back to prison as they knew no other way of life than committing crimes. He was free from his old strictly lawyer-style life and would have to find some new pathways for the next five years before he returned to it with a totally different attitude. Nevertheless, as a good citizen he did wonder whether all the public money spent on his arrest, trial and imprisonment had really been to the benefit of the public. He often thought about his own case and felt that if he was faced with a similar situation again he would probably do the same thing again but back up his actions with a formal Notice to Quit!

THE END

Breinigsville, PA USA
11 March 2011
257451BV00001B/56/P